GRAY GHOST
THE R.M.S. QUEEN MARY AT WAR

D1616272

The **Queen Mary** *receives a tumultuous welcome in New York at the conclusion of her maiden voyage, May 1936.*

The Cunard Line

GRAY GHOST

THE R.M.S. QUEEN MARY AT WAR

STEVE HARDING

PICTORIAL HISTORIES PUBLISHING COMPANY
MISSOULA, MONTANA

LIBRARY OF CONGRESS
CATALOG CARD NUMBER 82-61738

ISBN 0-933126-26-3

First Printing November 1982
Second Printing June 1986
Third Printing May 1995
Fourth Printing March 1999

Layout by Stan Cohen, Missoula, Montana
Typography by Arrow Graphics, Missoula, Montana
Cover Art Work by Mary Beth Percival, Missoula, Montana

FRONT COVER: The Queen Mary *bound for Scotland with a full load of G.I.s in 1943.*
Public Archives of Canada (#REA 253-115)

BACK COVER: The Queen Mary *entering New York Harbor just after V.E. Day.*
U.S. Army Transportation Museum

PICTORIAL HISTORIES PUBLISHING COMPANY
713 South Third West
Missoula, Montana 59801

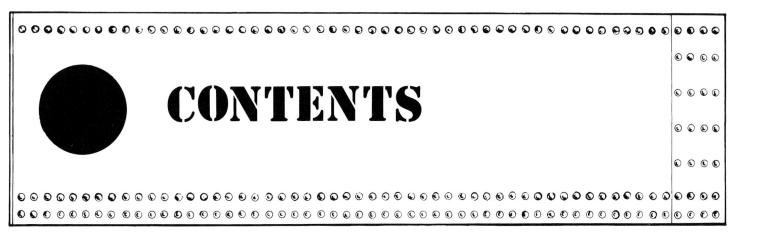

CONTENTS

The birth of a monarch: RMS Queen Mary *under construction at Clydebank, 1935.*   John Brown Engineering, Ltd.

INTRODUCTION

The widespread economic crisis that struck the world's major industrialized nations in the aftermath of the First World War hit Great Britain especially hard, and by the dawn of the 1920s unemployment and commercial decline were rampant throughout the United Kingdom. The nation's maritime industries were particularly vulnerable, and the shipping lines of France, Italy, Germany and the United States soon began to erode Britain's traditional dominance of the world's sea-borne cargo and passenger trade.

For the Cunard Steamship Company, long the United Kingdom's leading shipping line, the continuing decline in Britain's maritime fortunes was most apparent on the lucrative North Atlantic passenger routes. Cunard's premier express liners, the *Aquitania, Mauretania* and *Berengaria,* were simply too old to successfully compete with the newer and larger vessels being built in Europe and the United States. The firm was thus being slowly edged out of its most profitable market and, unless something was done quickly to reverse this alarming trend, the line would soon find itself at the point of economic no return.

Cunard's board of directors realized that the solution to the firm's problem was twofold. First, to remain competitive the company would obviously have to supplement its existing fleet with ships that could match or surpass the performance of the latest European and American superliners. And, second, Cunard would attempt to avoid the cost of building several huge, ornate and expensive vessels by instituting a Southampton-Cherbourg-New York service built around just two liners. If these ships were of comparable size and speed they could, by maintaining a weekly shuttle service, double revenues and reduce costs by eliminating the need for any additional liners.

Cunard's Technical Committee began preliminary development work on the first of the two new ships early in 1926. It was an awesome task, and the firm's engineers and naval architects were faced with a myriad of details. To be economically feasible the liner would have to carry at least 1700 passengers, as well as some 1200 crew members, at a minimum service speed of 27 knots. She must be able to maintain that speed for six days at a time, and would thus require absolute mechanical reliability coupled with excellent fuel economy. The ship would also have to be stable in all sea and weather conditions if she were to keep up the hectic schedule envisioned for her and, lastly, she must be able to offer her passengers the luxury that was Cunard's trademark.

The actual design of the new liner took almost four years to complete and, when finished in the spring of 1930, depicted a ship of truly awesome proportions. She was to be the largest merchant vessel yet built, with an overall length of 1019 feet and a gross weight of 81,000 tons. Her twelve decks would provide ample room for 2030 Cabin, Tourist, and Third-class passengers as well as 1280 crew members and 45,000 cubic feet of cargo. The liner's 24 oil-fired watertube boilers would produce a total of 160,000 shaft horsepower through four sets of single reduction geared turbines, turning her four 35-ton screws at three revolutions per second and thus giving the ship a projected service speed of 28.5 knots. Cunard's engineers estimated that the huge liner would burn a surprisingly economical 1000 tons of fuel oil every 24 hours while at sea, and allocated space for 8600 tons of the precious fluid. And, with the tragic example of the *Titanic* firmly in mind, the designers provided the ship with 24 lifeboats, 20 of which were diesel-powered and capable of carrying 145 people each.

In May 1930 Cunard announced that John Brown and Company had been selected to construct the new liner. The firm was an internationally-known builder of warships and merchant vessels, and its huge shipyard at Clydebank, Scotland, was perfectly suited to the construction of the world's first superliner. After arranging insurance coverage for the vessel, and for the building of docking and maintenance facilities in Southampton, Cherbourg and New York, Cunard was free to sign a firm contract with John Brown. This was done in November 1930, and construction of what the British press was already calling the "ultimate ship" began in Clydebank on December first. Work on the giant liner progressed rapidly over the next 11 months, and by November 1931 the nearly completed hull towered over the shipyard, its mere presence a comfort in those times of increasing economic crisis.

But as the winter wore on it became apparent that the new Cunarder was in serious trouble. British earnings in the maritime passenger trade had dropped more than 50 percent in the years between 1928 and 1931 and Cunard, despite optimistic reports to its shareholders, was finding it increasingly difficult to support the costs of the new liner. The future that had seemed so bright barely a year before now appeared bleak indeed, and there were rumors that work on hull number 534 was about to be halted. On December 11, 1931, the rumors became fact. One year and £1.5 million into the job, Cunard was forced to suspend construction on its superliner.

For the next two and a half years John Brown's Clydebank shipyard resembled a ghost town, with the abandoned carcass of hull 534 the only reminder of more prosperous times. Then, in November 1932, a ray of hope appeared on the horizon in the form of Chancellor of the Exchequer Neville Chamberlain. Mr. Chamberlain had long advocated the creation of a consolidated British shipping line that, with government support, could successfully compete with Europe's nationally subsidized fleets. Cunard's financial difficulties were matched by those of Britain's White Star line, and the Chancellor saw project 534 as a lever which could be used to bring about a merger between the two shipping companies, and thereby establish a strong British firm in the lucrative North Atlantic passenger trade.

At Mr. Chamberlain's urging the British Government thus offered the two ailing companies over £9 million in low-interest subsidies on condition that they join forces. Cunard would retain a controlling interest in the new firm, to be known as the Cunard-White Star line, and the subsidies would guarantee the completion of hull 534 and her planned sister ship. Though some Britons questioned the wisdom of the plan in light of the nation's other pressing economic needs Cunard and White Star did not, and the North Atlantic Shipping (Advances) Bill was approved by Parliament on March 27, 1934.

Work on hull 534 resumed almost immediately after the Cunard-White Star merger, and the Royal Mail Steamer Queen Mary was launched at Clydebank on September 26, 1934. For the next 18 months the liner lay in John Brown's huge fitting out basin, where swarms of workers labored around the clock to install the engines, fittings and furnishings that would guarantee the ship's position as the world's ultimate express liner. By March of 1936 the Queen Mary could rightfully claim that

title, for with her five dining areas, five lounges, two cocktail bars, two swimming pools, grand ballroom, squash court and small but well-equipped hospital, she was as much a posh resort as she was a ship.

Following the successful completion of her sea trials the Queen Mary was made ready for her maiden voyage, which she began in Southampton on May 27, 1936 surrounded by all the pomp and circumstance befitting a national symbol. She did not, however, end this first voyage with a return of the trans-Atlantic speed record to Britain's possession. In fact, on her maiden crossing the United Kingdom's expensive and much-vaunted symbol of maritime supremacy revealed several rather serious design deficiencies. Her propellors, for example, caused severe vibrations throughout the ship and the liner showed an alarming tendency to roll quite a bit even in moderate seas. The vessel's funnels showered passengers and crew with soot, her plumbing and electrical systems failed, and tortured groans emanating from her hull pointed to serious flaws in her inner frame.

Though Cunard-White Star went to great lengths to correct these problems with stop-gap measures, it was soon obvious that nothing less than a comprehensive rebuild would suffice. So, less than a year after her maiden voyage, the Queen Mary was withdrawn from service and sent to Southampton for a complete overhaul. During this period the liner's hull was strengthened, her funnels were equipped with smoke filters and her plumbing and electrical systems were thoroughly examined and repaired. And, finally, her original screws were replaced by four manganese-bronze propellors specially designed to eliminate vibration.

This extensive refit transformed the Queen Mary into a stable and dependable mount, and she vindicted herself in August 1936 by returning the fabled Blue Ribband to Britain after a record Atlantic crossing of less than four days. For the next three years the ship criss-crossed the North Atlantic, the undisputed Queen of the express liners. Her luxury and elegance became world famous, and the elite of several continents soon came to consider her the only civilized way to travel.

In those halcyon days of shipboard galas and sumptuous banquets, of celebrity passengers and trans-Atlantic speed records, the growing crisis in Europe seemed far away indeed. Most of the Queen Mary's privileged passengers considered Adolph Hitler a posturing boor, and paid scant attention to the momentous events taking place in Berlin, Munich, Prague and Warsaw. But the storm clouds of war were clearly gathering on the horizon, and they would soon unleash a tempest that even the "ultimate ship" would be unable to avoid.

CHAPTER ONE:
THE QUEEN CALLED UP

The outbreak of the Second World War on September 3, 1939, found the RMS *Queen Mary* nearing the end of her 143rd Atlantic crossing. She had sailed from Southampton four days earlier with a record 2332 passengers aboard, the vast majority of whom were Americans hoping to escape the general European holocaust that suddenly seemed inevitable.

Under normal circumstances the liner's bridge crew would already have sighted the Ambrose lightship that marked the outer approaches to New York Harbor, but normal routine had no place on this voyage. The clouds of war that had been gathering over Europe since the Munich Conference had darkened considerably in the last days of August, and shortly before the Cunarder's departure from Southampton the British Admiralty had directed all United Kingdom merchant vessels to henceforth avoid their regular trade routes. The *Queen Mary* was thus almost 100 miles south of her usual track, racing west at more than 28 knots.

Other safety measures were in force as well. Shortly before midnight on September 2nd the *Queen's* master had received a coded Admiralty message directing him to put his ship on full war alert. He was ordered to take "all necessary precautions" to ensure the liner's safe arrival in New York, and was to give "particular attention to the threat of submarine attack." Work crews armed with paint and brushes had immediately begun the monumental task of blacking out the *Queen's* 2000 portholes and windows, and the surrounding sea had gone dark as the liner's exterior lights were extinguished. Additional lookouts had been posted to scan the horizon for potentially hostile forces, and the helmsman had been ordered to steer a zigzag course meant to make the Cunarder as difficult a target as possible.

Now, with war a dire reality, the *Queen Mary* sailed on across a sea quite possibly teeming with enemies. Groups of anxious passengers gathered around loudspeakers broadcasting the latest news from London, and an atmosphere of tense anticipation dampened the normally festive mood in the liner's public rooms. Few of those aboard that night could forget the tragic sinking of the *Lusitania* dur-

ing the First World War, for it was a grim reminder of the fate that awaited any passenger vessel attacked without warning on the high seas. And, as the most prestigious and visible symbol of Britain's maritime might, the *Queen Mary* would undoubtedly be a prime target for every German ship on the North Atlantic.

But the remainder of the *Queen's* voyage was mercifully uneventful, and she arrived safely in New York on the morning of September 5th. The Admiralty had directed all liners of United Kingdom registry to remain in whatever friendly or neutral ports they found themselves, and on September 6th the Cunard-White Star office in New York cancelled all further sailings of the *Queen Mary* "for the foreseeable future." The ship thus began a period of forced hibernation at Pier 90 on the Hudson River, moored near the interned French liner *Normandie*. The majority of the Cunarder's crew immediately returned to vital war jobs in Britain, and by September 10th only a small maintenance party remained aboard.

A few weeks after her arrival, however, the *Queen Mary's* ranks began to swell with the members of a special British Intelligence security team. The huge liner was a tempting target for Axis saboteurs, and a combined British-American effort had been organized to protect her. The FBI and the New York Police Department, as well as the U.S. Army, Navy and Coast Guard, joined forces with the British agents to ensure the *Queen's* safety. Scores of floodlights were set up to sweep the ship after dark, and armed guards began patrolling both the liner and her pier around the clock. Inactive the *Queen Mary* might be, but her guardians were determined that her forced stay in New York would be a quiet one.

Early on the morning of March 7, 1940, Cunard-White Star's other superliner appeared in New York. The RMS *Queen Elizabeth* had been launched at Clydebank in 1938, but the outbreak of war had interrupted her final fitting-out. She had therefore never entered service, and had lain uncompleted in the River Clyde until the British Government realized what a sitting duck she was. The Admiralty then ordered the ship to the relative safety of the

United States, and she had left Scotland for New York on March 2nd. Upon arrival she tied up at Cunard's pier on the Hudson, only a few yards from the *Queen Mary,* and settled in for what promised to be a long stay.

The *Queen Elizabeth's* appearance in New York marked the first time that both Cunard's superliners had been in the same port at the same time, and they made quite a sight. The *Queen Mary,* still resplendent in her peacetime red, white and black livery, contrasted sharply with the *Queen Elizabeth's* coat of camouflage gray. Though only a few years older, the *Mary* was obviously of a different generation with her vast array of topside louvres and exhaust ventilators, while the *Elizabeth* had a much more modern streamlined look. Ironically, the *Queen Mary* would always be the faster of the two despite her age and less businesslike mien.

While the Cunard *Queens* sat idle in New York a heated debate over their ultimate fate raged in London. Britain's increasingly dismal military fortunes made the need for troopships alarmingly apparent, yet several members of His Majesty's Government argued that the *Queens* were simply not suited to the dangers of wartime service. The ships were, their critics charged, "white elephants" whose very size would make them the objects of constant enemy attention. It was logical to assume that Nazi Germany would make every effort to locate and sink what were potentially the world's largest troopships, and Britain simply could not spare the ships and men necessary to protect the *Queens* at sea. Furthermore, the argument ran, the liners could not even be used as cargo ships for, despite their size, they could provide space for only a few hundred tons of foodstuffs or military hardware. Finally, the 1000 tons of fuel oil each ship would

The coming of war ended the rivalry between France's premier liner, the Normandie, *and Britain's* Queen Mary, *seen here moored next to each other in New York, September 1939. The* Normandie *was seized by the United States government after the fall of France, and was intended for use as an American troopship. But, while undergoing conversion, the vessel caught fire and sank at her mooring on February 10, 1942.*

Library of Congress

burn in a 24-hour period could be put to better use by the ships of the Royal Navy. The liners' critics concluded their arguments by suggesting that the Cunard *Queens* would be more valuable to the war effort as sources of scrap metal than as troopships.

But the liners had supporters as well as detractors in the highest levels of the British Government, and the arguments in favor of requisitioning the *Queens* for trooping duty received increasingly favorable attention as the months passed. Britain's more realistic leaders knew that the "phony war" that had enveloped Europe after the German invasion of Poland was only the calm before the Teutonic storm, and argued that the giant ships would be essential for transporting badly needed reinforcements from the far-flung nations of the Commonwealth to the Home Islands. The *Queens'* advocates pointed out that the size of the liners was actually a positive factor, in that each ship would be able to carry large numbers of troops over vast distances, using routes that smaller and less sturdy vessels could not safely navigate. More importantly, the Cunarders were much faster than any other troopship then in use and, if operated on the

sort of shuttle service for which they had originally been designed, would prove more economically practical than smaller ships. The *Queens'* speed would also allow them to outrun almost any existing Axis warship, thus eliminating the need for escorts and freeing the hard-pressed Royal Navy for service elsewhere. And, finally, the more pragmatic members of His Majesty's Government reasoned that, even if the *Queens* should eventually be lost on military service, the money used to operate them as troopships would be better spent than that used to maintain them idle in New York.

Those in favor of using the Cunarders as troop transports eventually won out, and the Admiralty decided that the already proven *Queen Mary* would be the first of the two liners to be "called up." The official requisition note, delivered to Cunard-White Star in March 1940, stated that

His Majesty's Government relies on the goodwill of yourselves, your staffs and agents in carrying out these instructions and preparing the ship for the King's service, especially as regards clearing cargo, fuelling, storring and manning.

Cunard's second superliner, RMS Queen Elizabeth, *had been launched at Clyde Bank in 1938 but the outbreak of war had interrupted her final fitting out. The huge ship lay uncompleted in the River Clyde until ordered to New York in March 1940. In this photo the liner is seen moving slowly down the River Clyde, bound for New York and, ultimately, her trooping partnership with the* Queen Mary. A.C. McNaught

RMS Queen Elizabeth *(foreground), shortly after her arrival in New York, March 7, 1940. The* Queen Mary *is moored just on the other side of Cunard's Pier 90, and the uncamouflaged* Normandie *stands out sharply just beyond. The smaller, two-stacked ship to starboard of the French liner is Cunard's* Mauretania.

A similar note concerning the *Queen Elizabeth* was to follow shortly, as would requisitions for 16 other Cunard-White Star vessels. In all, the British Government would eventually impress over 430,000 tons of the Line's shipping during the war.

For the remainder of March workmen in New York labored day and night to prepare the *Queen Mary* for her first military voyage. As the days passed her well-known Cunard colors disappeared beneath a hastily applied coat of camouflage gray, and the huge letters spelling out her name on bow and stern were obscured to guarantee her future anonymity. Cunard-White Star also ordered most of the liner's luxury appointments off-loaded in New York in preparation for the actual trooping conversion that was to take place in Australia. Several miles of plush Wilton carpeting were therefore removed from the *Queen Mary's* public rooms and passageways, her more fragile fittings were dismantled and crated, and over 200 cases of crystal, china and silverware were packed for storage. These items, along with much of the ship's better furniture, would spend the duration of the war in Cunard's warehouses along the Hudson.

The admiralty was reasonably certain the *Queen Mary* could evade even the most determined Axis submarines, but the liner's New York militarization nonetheless included the installation of an ASDIC underwater sound detection system. And, though the *Mary's* great speed would be her best defense against enemy surface raiders, London insisted a single four-inch gun be mounted on the ship's fantail. The weapon would prove woefully inadequate if matched against the 11-inchers of a German pocket battleship, but would provide some protection if the liner were attacked by smaller vessels. This same rationale determined the extent of the Cunarder's anti-aircraft defenses as well; the few World War I vintage Lewis and Vickers machine guns installed aboard the ship would not deter a large-scale attack, but could deal effectively with the lone reconnaissance plane the liner might accidentally encounter. And, lastly, the *Queen Mary* was equipped with a degaussing girdle meant to neutralize magnetic mines.

On the morning of March 19, 1940, the *Queen's* master was summoned to the Line's offices in midtown Manhattan. There Captain R.B. Irving was informed that his ship must be ready to sail within 48 hours, and that she would make for Sydney by way of Trinidad, Cape Town, and the western Australia port of Freemantle. That afternoon the liner's skeleton crew was fleshed out with 470 officers and men from the Cunarder *Antonia,* and the difficult task of preparing the *Queen Mary* for sea began. Observant harbor workers noticed increased activity around the supposedly dormant vessel that evening, with lifeboats being tested and stronger security patrols in evidence on the pier.

Public speculation about the *Queen Mary's* status intensified on March 20th following the unannounced evening departure of the Cunard liner *Mauretania*. The vessel, also destined for trooping conversion in Australia, had slipped quietly down the Hudson hidden by fog and a driving rain. British Intelligence hoped that New York's resident community of Axis spies would believe the activity aboard the *Queen Mary* had only been a cover for the departure of the smaller and less easily recognized *Mauretania*. If this double deception worked as planned, German forces would concentrate their attention on the *Mauretania,* and the *Queen Mary* would thus be safe from all but a chance encounter with enemy units.

Just after eight o'clock on the morning of March 21st a group of tugs edged the *Queen Mary* out into the Hudson and pointed her downstream. Smoke poured from the liner's three funnels as she moved slowly toward the open sea, her escort of Coast Guard and NYPD launches leading the way. The New York correspondent of the *London Times* later reported that thousands of commuters "waved to the liner and a few clapped their hands, but there were no other demonstrations, and from the *Queen Mary* there was no sign..." Once in the open Atlantic the huge liner turned south and was gone.

During the next few days newspapers in the United States and Great Britain wondered openly about the ultimate destinations of both the *Queen Mary* and *Mauretania*. On March 23rd the *Times of London* reported that

> There are all sorts of speculations and rumours about the vessels and their errands... The *Mauretania* has not been reported since she left harbour, but the *Queen Mary* was sighted off Longbranch, New Jersey, just before noon yesterday headed southwards, and because of that it is believed that she is going to the naval station at Bermuda to have her hull cleansed of barnacles...

Two days later the *New York Sun* reported that it had learned, "on the highest authority," that both the *Queen Mary* and *Mauretania*

> ...will become vital links in Canada's huge air training programme, carrying men and supplies between Australia and western Canada. In Australia they will take on air cadets, who have gone through the preliminary stages of their training there and who will be given their advanced schooling in Canada. They will be able to cut to the minimum the time consumed in moving cadets from the flying fields of Australia to those of Canada. There will doubtless be a need for shipping training planes and other supplies back to Australia from Canada, so it will not be an entirely one-way job for the big liners. It would be relatively safe to use the luxury ships for such work. Their chances of being waylaid either by submarines or pocket battleships on the run between Sydney and Vancouver would be extremely remote.

The chances of the *Queen Mary* being attacked on the Australia-western Canada run were remote indeed, for it was a route she would never travel. His Majesty's Government had quite a different military career in mind for the *Queen Mary,* a career that would begin as soon as her trooping conversion was completed. Then, and only then, would the giant Cunarder take to the sea as a ship of war.

British Intelligence hoped that Axis agents would notice the March 20, 1940 departure from New York of the Cunarder Mauretania, *while missing the* Queen Mary's *departure the next day. The plan worked, and the* Queen Mary *was thus able to safely reach Australia. The* Mauretania *was herself converted for trooping duties, and is seen here in San Francisco in 1943.*

U.S. Naval Historical Center

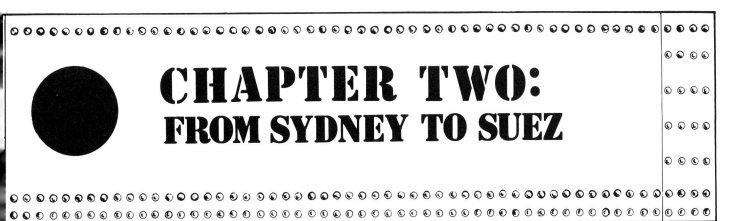

CHAPTER TWO:
FROM SYDNEY TO SUEZ

The *Queen Mary* arrived safely off Sydney Head on April 17th, after a voyage of more than 14,000 miles made at an average speed of 27.2 knots. The next day she was moved to the Cockatoo Docks and Engineering Company's pier, and her metamorphosis from luxury liner to troopship began in earnest under the watchful eyes of Cunard technicians dispatched from London.

The *Queen's* conversion was a Herculean task in all respects. Most of her remaining furnishings, and over 2000 stateroom doors, were removed and packed off to local warehouses for the duration. Tiers of wooden bunks and rows of canvas hammocks soon appeared throughout the ship, her galleys and heads were enlarged, and most of the shops in the ship's Main Hall were converted into military offices. Workmen welded hinged steel blast shutters over the liner's bridge windows, and hundreds of sandbags were brought aboard to protect vital areas of her superstructure. In just two short weeks the *Queen Mary* was transformed into the largest and fastest troopship the world had yet seen, capable of hauling 5000 men and most of their equipment around the globe at a speed of 30 knots.

Her conversion completed, the *Queen* was at last ready to begin her trooping career. On the morning of May 4, 1940 the liner left Sydney in company with the converted Cunarders *Aquitania* and *Mauretania,* the Canadian Pacific liners *Empress of Japan, Empress of Britain* and *Empress of Canada,* and the RMS *Andes.* The group, escorted by the Australian cruisers HMAS *Australia* and HMAS *Canberra,* called briefly at Freemantle to take on provisions and additional troops and, on May 10th, set out on the 6,000-mile journey across the Indian Ocean to Cape Town.

Sixteen days later the convoy dropped anchor in Table Bay. The voyage to South Africa had been long and nerve-wracking, and the crews of the seven troopships hoped for a few days of well-deserved rest. But early that same evening the Royal Navy representative in Cape Town informed the convoy's senior officers that the liners must be ready to sail again within 24 hours. They would be joined at Simonstown by the escorting cruiser HMS *Cumberland, Australia* and *Canberra* being needed elsewhere, and were to make for the Clyde "with all possible speed."

The Admiralty's plea for a rapid passage was understandable given the increasingly bleak Allied position in Europe. Nazi Germany had conquered Denmark and invaded Norway the previous month, and on May 10th the Wehrmacht had smashed into Holland, Belgium and Luxembourg, rendering the vaunted Maginot Line useless simply by passing around its nearly unprotected left flank. Three days later German armored units, striking through the supposedly impenetrable Ardennes forests, drove a wedge between the overwhelmed Allied armies and trapped the British Expeditionary Forces in Belgium and northern France. The successful Dunkirk evacuation saved the BEF from certain destruction, but the retreating British units were forced to abandon much of their equipment and most of their heavy weapons on the beaches. The badly mauled units returning to England would thus be hard pressed to repel the German invasion of the Home Islands that was now sure to come, and the 14,000 Australian and New Zealand troops aboard the *Queen Mary* and her companions were desperately needed to bolster the United Kingdom's sagging defenses.

The liners stayed in South Africa only long enough to take on fuel and provisions, setting sail for Scotland on May 28th. But the situation in Europe continued to deteriorate even as the ships raced for the Clyde. On June 8th all remaining Allied troops were evacuated from Norway. Two days later Italy declared war on Britain and France, and Italian troops crossed the French frontier on a front stretching from Switzerland to the Mediterranean. Paris fell to the Wehrmacht on June 14th, and the following day Premier Paul Reynaud informed the British Government that France could no longer honor her pledge to refuse a separate peace with Germany. On June 16th, the same day that the *Queen Mary* and her retinue dropped anchor at Clydebank, Marshal Philippe Petain replaced Reynaud as Premier and appealed to Berlin for an immediate armistice.

The welcome accorded the *Queen Mary* upon her arrival in Scotland was warm, though understandably restrained given the worsening news from the Continent. The people of the Clyde had a proprietary interest in "their" liner, and her safe return after a six-year absence was cause for celebration. But the festive atmosphere was dampened by the knowledge that Great Britain was now facing one of the most dangerous periods in her long history. The final conquest of France assured Germany's complete mastery of Europe, and Adolph Hitler could now be expected to unleash the full fury of the Nazi blitzkrieg against the United Kingdom.

The British Government realized that the nation's only hope for survival lay in the swift arrival of reinforcements from the Commonwealth countries. The speed and passenger capacity of the *Queen Mary* and her fellow liners thus dramatically increased their value to the war effort after the French capitulation, but at the same time guaranteed that they would be relentlessly hunted by every means at Hitler's command. Indeed, the frequency of German attacks on Allied troopships had already begun to increase, with six large troopers having gone to the bottom during the French and Norwegian campaigns alone. Still, the remaining troopships would have to soldier on no matter what the cost, for it was imperative that their vital human cargoes reach the battlefields.

Australian troops aboard the Queen Mary *published their own newspaper, the* Ammo Daily. *This issue was published during voyage WW#2, by and for troops of the Australian 6th Division.*   The Wrather Corporation

Tasmanians of the Australian 7th Division embarked aboard Queen Mary *pose for a group portrait,*
October 1940.

Australian War Memorial

Lord Gowrie inspects Australian nurses embarked aboard Queen Mary, *December 1940.*

Another Australian group portrait, taken aboard Queen Mary *in Sydney Harbor, December 1940.*

Captain R.B. Irving was well aware of the hazards that would face the *Queen Mary* on the high seas and, like most of his crew, had heard the rumor that the liner was a "marked ship." According to the scuttlebutt circulating on the Clydebank waterfront, Hitler had offered a reward of $250,000.00 and the Iron Cross with oak leaves to any U-boat captain that could sink the Cunarder. Yet there was danger, too, even in the relative safety of port. Luftwaffe reconnaissance aircraft had begun to show a keen interest in ships plying the Firth of Clyde, and German spies active in Scotland were known to be particularly interested in the activities of the *Queen Mary.*

But British Intelligence was working equally hard to protect the great liner. The ship's crew was repeatedly reminded of the need for absolute security, and those few sailors that spoke a bit too freely while relaxing at local pubs soon found themselves transferred to duties ashore. Local newspapers were informed that stiff penalties would follow the publication of any information concerning the *Queen Mary's* movements, and

photographers that found the ship an interesting subject were promptly detained and their film confiscated. Armed troops continued their around-the-clock patrols of the ship and her pier, and even the most routine shipboard maintenance was performed under the watchful eyes of security personnel. These stringent precautions, though seen as excessive by some, were necessary for the security of the nation as well as the safety of the *Queen Mary*; Great Britain's troopship capacity would be reduced by almost 20 percent should the giant Cunarder be sunk or severely damaged.

Fortunately, no harm came to the ship during her fortnight's sojourn on the Clyde and, on the morning of June 28, 1940, Captain Irving was ordered to prepare the liner for sea. The *Queen Mary's* crew was recalled from shore leave, workmen labored throughout the night to load fuel and provisions, and shortly after dawn the next day the ship once again set a course for the open Atlantic. Captain Irving's sealed orders, opened only after the liner had cleared the Firth of Clyde, directed him to make for Singapore via Cape Town

The Queen Mary *passing Bradley Head, Sydney, bound for Freemantle and Trincomalee, December 28, 1940. Though the liner's movements were supposed to be secret, her arrivals and departures were always accompanied by a flotilla of small boats and waving civilians.* Australian War Memorial (#5579)

Cape Town was a regular port of call for the Queen Mary *during her Australia-Middle East service, and she is seen here anchored in Table Bay in July 1940. In the left foreground is the bow of the South African training ship* General Botha *(ex-HMS* Thames*), and the Cunarder* Aquitania *can be seen to the right of* Queen Mary.

and Trincomalee, Ceylon. After a much needed drydocking at Britain's huge Asian naval base the ship would return to Sydney to resume her trooping duties.

The 14,000-mile voyage to Singapore was uneventful, and the *Queen Mary* entered the port's giant drydock on August fifth. For the next 41 days the ship was a scene of constant activity, as workmen swarmed over her from stem to stern. The crust of barnacles that had collected on her hull was removed, her steering gear and engineroom machinery were overhauled, and she received another coat of camouflage gray. The liner was also fitted with a minesweeping paravane system consisting of two torpedo-shaped devices attached by long cables to a winch on the forwardmost point of her bow. When towed underwater on either side of the vessel, the paravanes would cut the mooring cables of submerged mines, which would then float harmlessly to the surface to be destroyed by gunfire. The system was meant to compliment her degaussing girdle and would give her the complete protection against mines that her speed alone could not guarantee.

The liner's stay in Singapore gave her crew a much needed opportunity to unwind after their long and anxious voyage, and they did so with a vengeance. Indeed, the city's police force had its hands full attempting to keep the rowdier members of the ship's company from dismantling the waterfront bar district brick by brick. The local military commander was on the verge of restricting all crewmembers to the ship when, on September 14th, the Italian invasion of Egypt brought an abrupt end to the frivolity. The attack was a stunning blow to Britain, for it raised the spectre of an Axis offensive aimed at the Suez Canal. Such an assault would, if successful, cut the United Kingdom's vital supply lines to Australia and India, and at the same time pave the way for an Axis conquest of the oil-rich Middle East.

Thus, almost overnight, the Mediterranean became the principal theater of war. His Majesty's Government immediately directed that all available reinforcements be rushed to Egypt despite the continuing threat of a German invasion of the Home Islands, and the *Queen Mary* was ordered to cut short her stay in Singapore and pro-

The Queen Mary *departing Sydney in April 1941, bound for Suez with a load of Anzacs.*

Australian troops prepare for debarkation in Singapore in the spring of 1941. These troops would soon be called upon to help defend the city against attacking Japanese forces, a defense that would fail despite the Australians' presence.

The Queen Elizabeth *(foreground) and* Queen Mary *meet at sea for the first time, off Sydney Head, April 1941.*
Australian War Memorial (#7959)

Queen Mary, Queen Elizabeth, Mauretania *and* Nieuw Amsterdam *in convoy in Australian waters, April 1941.*
Australian War Memorial (#106027)

ceed to Sydney "with the greatest possible speed." The liner arrived in Australia on September 25th and, following three weeks additional work meant to further increase her trooping capacity, began ferrying troops toward the Middle East on October 20th.

For the next seven months the *Queen Mary* crisscrossed the Indian Ocean, sometimes alone and sometimes in convoy. The Admiralty had decided that she would make far too tempting a target in the confines of the Red Sea, so the liner was allowed to travel no farther than Bombay or Trincomalee. There her troops were transferred to smaller vessels for the voyage to Suez, while the Cunarder returned to Australia for another load.

While the *Queen Mary* was thus engaged the *Queen Elizabeth* was being readied for her own trooping debut. Cunard's second superliner had been requisitioned following the Italian invasion of Egypt and, following conversion in Singapore and

Sydney, was ready to enter service by the end of March. The two great liners sailed together for the first time in early April when, accompanied by the *Mauretania*, they carried 10,000 Australian and New Zealand troops all the way to Suez.

The Cunard Queens continued their shuttle service between Australia and the Middle East for the remainder of 1941, and it was a trying time for the crews of both ships. Though the presence of German submarines and surface raiders in the Indian Ocean and Red Sea approaches kept the liners on constant alert, it was the sweltering heat that proved a greater menace. The Queens had been designed to operate in the frigid North Atlantic, and had thus never been fitted with air conditioning. As a result, temperatures in the lower deck areas often soared into the hundreds under the harsh Indian Ocean sun, and the troops crowded aboard like cattle suffered terrible hardships. Despite sea water showers and other preventative

The Queen Mary *in Trincomalee Harbor, July 1941, as seen by the noted Australian artist F. Norton.*

Australian War Memorial (#9653)

measures several soldiers died of heat exhaustion during the summer of 1941, and the brutal conditions caused several near mutinies.

The troop transport program continued at full speed despite the difficulties, however, and by the end of November the Cunard Queens had carried some 80,000 ANZACs to Europe and the Middle East. The efforts of the *Queen Mary* and *Queen Elizabeth* allowed Britain to stabilize her defense lines in North Africa, and thereby slow the Axis advance toward Egypt. And though the situation in the Middle East was by no means secure, some war planners had begun to predict that 1942 might be the "year of decision" in the war against Nazi Germany and her Allies.

But any hopes of a quick end to the war were shattered by the devastating Japanese attack on Pearl Harbor in December 1941. The destruction of the American Pacific Fleet, and Tokyo's subsequent declaration of war against the Allies, radically altered Great Britain's strategic planning. Until December 7th British shipping had travelled the Pacific almost at will, the only danger being that of attack by a single far-ranging German U-boat or surface raider. But Japan's entry into the war on the Axis side now threatened Britain's vital supply line to Australia and the Indian sub-continent, and the safe haven afforded the ships of the Royal Navy at Singapore and Hong Kong might at any moment turn into a death trap should Japanese troops strike southward from their bases in China.

An even more serious threat lay in the danger of a Japanese attack aimed at Australia. The mass movement of ANZAC troops to Europe and the Middle East had drastically weakened the island continent's defenses, and the Allied forces remaining in the southern Pacific would be hard pressed to repel a Japanese thrust launched from Indonesia or New Guinea. And, should Australia fall, the Axis would dominate the Pacific and Indian Oceans, threaten India and East Africa, and completely sever the flow of oil and rubber so essential to the Allied war effort.

The escorting cruiser HMAS Sydney *leads* Queen Mary *(center right) and* Queen Elizabeth *past Wilson's Promontory, coast of Victoria, Australia, during the summer of 1941.*

Australian War Memorial (#128094)

Ile de France *(right) and* Queen Mary *at rest in Sydney, early 1942.*

Australian War Memorial (#133576)

But Japan's attack on the United States had its positive aspects as well, for it brought the United States into the Second World War on the Allied side. President Franklin D. Roosevelt had long believed that America would one day have to join the battle against the Axis, both to forestall a German conquest of Great Britain and as an act of national self-defense, and he had secretly collaborated with Prime Minister Winston Churchill on a joint strategy for the defeat of both Nazi tyranny and Japanese expansionism. But isolationist sentiments were strong in the United States, and Roosevelt had been unable to offer more than token support to the beleaguered British.

The devastation of Pearl Harbor, though one of the most brilliant operations in modern military history, was therefore a grave error on Japan's part. The last vestiges of American isolationism disappeared in the flames of Battleship Row, and the sleeping giant of the United States' industrial and military might was awakened from its long slumber. It would take time, of course, for the "arsenal of democracy" to gear up for full production, but the alliance of Great Britain and the United States against fascism was assured. It was a partnership in which the *Queen Mary* was destined to play a major role.

Australian nurses and VADs debark from Queen Mary *via lighter, Sydney, March 1943.*

Australian War Memorial (#29487)

Australian walking wounded return home from the Middle East, March 1943, courtesy of His Majesty's Transport Queen Mary.

Australian War Memorial (#29483)

Troops of the Australian 9th Division returning from duty in the Middle East get a nice view of the Queen Mary's *famous profile, March 1943.* Australian War Memorial (#50276)

CHAPTER THREE:
CAUGHT IN THE DRAFT

The outbreak of war in the Pacific found the *Queen Mary* riding safely at anchor in Trincomalee, Ceylon. The liner had been enroute to Singapore for a refit intended to increase her troop capacity, but the widespread Japanese offensive that followed the attack on Pearl Harbor made such a journey impossible. Japanese troops had already begun to advance down the Malay Peninsula toward Singapore and the oil-rich Dutch East Indies, and the December 10th sinking of the British battleships *Prince of Wales* and *Repulse* by Japanese aircraft had clearly shown that no Allied vessel in the South Pacific or Indian Ocean was safe from aerial attack. The admiralty therefore ordered the valuable Cunarder to New York, and she set sail on December 19th.

The *Queen Mary* dropped anchor in the Hudson River on January 12, 1942 after a 12,000-mile voyage by way of Cape Town and Trinidad. It had been almost two years since the liner had been seen in New York, and she received a joyous welcome. Thousands of wildly cheering people jammed the West Side Highway, and the windows of buildings on 50th Street were filled with handkerchief-waving New Yorkers. The prevailing mood in the city was "whatever *Mary* wants, *Mary* gets," and the Red Cross was the first to oblige by supplying the ship's crew with the overcoats that had not been necessary during the liner's recent travels in the tropics.

But even as the *Queen Mary* was settling in for a much needed rest in New York, plans were being made in Washington for her future role in the Allied war effort. Winston Churchill and senior members of his staff had visited the United States in the last weeks of 1941, and the Cunard Queens had been a major topic in discussions with American war planners. Though Britain and the United States had agreed that the defeat of Nazi Germany was the first priority, it was alarmingly apparent that the situation in the Pacific required immediate Allied attention. After much discussion it was decided that the United States would supply the bulk of the men and materiel needed to halt the Japanese advance, while Britain would supply the ships necessary to carry the troops and their equipment to Australia. The Cunard Queens were the obvious choice to bear the brunt of this new trooping program, and were scheduled to begin the task as soon as modifictions needed to increase their trooping capacity were completed.

The *Queen Mary* thus entered drydock at the Boston Navy Yard on January 27, 1942, and for the next 13 days underwent a facelift that increased her troop capacity from 5,000 to 8,500. Workers from the Bethlehem Steel Company added several thousand standee bunks to those already aboard the liner, and the ship's promenade deck, swimming pool, and ladies' drawing room were soon packed with the narrow beds. Additional toilet facilities were added as well, and provision was made for storing the several hundred additional tons of food and water that would be consumed by the troops.

The *Queen Mary's* Boston refit also included the improvement of her armament. Throughout 1941 the liner had depended upon her modest number of Vickers and Lewis machineguns to protect her in case of aerial attack, and her single four-inch gun had originally been thought sufficient for defense against surfaced submarines. But the vulnerability of even heavily armed ships had been all too clearly pointed out at Pearl Harbor and on the North Atlantic convoy routes, and it was decided that the *Queen Mary* should have defenses equal to those of at least a light cruiser. The ship's anti-aircraft defenses were therefore supplemented with ten 40mm cannon in five double mounts sited fore and aft, as well as 24 single-barrel 20mm cannon emplaced in steel tub-mounts along the liner's upper superstructure. Six three-inch high/low angle guns were also installed, two forward of the bridge near the well deck and four mounted on the aft superstructure forward of the fantail. Finally, four sets of rather primitive two-inch anti-aircraft rocket launchers were grouped around the aft funnel.

With her refit completed the *Queen Mary* was ready to begin her first voyage with American troops aboard. Late on the night of February 17th 8,398 soldiers, most of them anti-aircraft artillerymen and ordnance troops, boarded the liner under cover of darkness. Fuelling and provisioning continued well into the next day, however, and the *Queen Mary* did not get underway until just after noon on the 18th. Then, under a bright blue sky, the ship headed northeast out of Boston until out of sight of land, when she altered course due south. Her route would take her to Sydney via Trinidad, Rio de Janeiro, Cape Town and Freemantle.

Increased U-boat activity near Trinidad forced the liner to divert to Key West, and it was there that Captain James Bisset took command of the *Queen Mary*. Bisset, a 35-year veteran of Cunard Service and future Commodore of the Line, replaced Captain R.B. Irving, who had reached mandatory retirement age. Captain Bisset later recalled that, on first sight, the liner's blurred outline in the fog

...gave her the appearance of a great rock set in the middle of the sea. Two U.S. destroyers were patrolling around the anchored ship, on the lookout for U-boats. As we drew nearer, I could make out two tankers, one moored on each side of her, amidships, feeding her with oil-fuel and fresh water. Though the tankers were vessels of 6,000 tons, they were dwarfed by her tremendous bulk. Gazing up at her...I felt overawed at the responsibility soon to be mine...

Soon after Captain Bisset came aboard the liner completd her provisioning and, with 8300 tons of fuel oil, 6500 tons of fresh water and 1000 tons of food aboard, was ready to resume her journey.

Captain Bisset set the ship on a course that took her on a western sweep around Cuba, then east into the Caribbean, and finally through the Anegada Passage into the Atlantic. The liner's master had no way of knowing that two German submarines, U-161, and U-129, were taking the same route. The

This photo of the Queen Mary's *stern, taken in New York in 1942, shows her two aft-mounted guns to good advantage. The weapons would prove woefully inadequate if matched against those of a German pocket battleship, but could well deal with the lone surfaced U-boat the* Queen *might encounter.*

presence of the German raiders did not remain a secret for long, however, for a few minutes after clearing the Passage the *Queen Mary's* radio operator picked up a distress call from a torpedoed Allied oil tanker. The ship, which had passed the Cunarder 45 minutes before, had encountered a U-boat only ten miles astern of the *Queen Mary*. It was the first of several close calls the liner would experience on the trip to Australia.

In Rio, where the *Queen Mary's* size forced her to anchor in the roads following her March 6th arrival, an Axis plot aimed at sinking her was already underway. A group of German and Italian spies, led by Count Edmondo Di Robilant, had somehow discovered the liner's sailing schedule and had broadcast this vital information to U-boats lurking off the Brazilian coast. The message was fortunately intercepted by Allied Intelligence, and Captain Bisset was directed to get the *Queen Mary* out of Rio several hours ahead of her scheduled sailing time. The ship's master kept her in port only long enough to take on fuel and provisions, and the Cunarder set out on the 3,300-mile journey to Cape Town on March 8th.

The *Queen Mary's* early departure from Rio quite probably saved her, for an oil tanker that left the port at the time the Cunard liner should have was sunk by a U-boat waiting in ambush a few miles offshore. The Germans had been so sure they would sink the *Queen Mary*, in fact, that Axis radio actually reported her destruction. The broadcast

UNITED STATES FORCE 5691 EAST

FEBRUARY - MARCH, 1942

The Queen Mary *embarked her first load of American troops in Boston on February 17, 1942, and carried them to Sydney via South America and South Africa. The U.S. Force Commander, Brig. Gen. Robert H. Van Volkenburgh, and his officers presented copies of this commemorative "Roll of American Officers Embarked" to Captain Bisset and his immediate staff as a memento of the voyage.* The Wrather Corporation

Close-up of the 3-inch gun mounted aft of the former Verandah Grill. This position also housed the liner's aft emergency steering gear, and the necessary engine order telegraphs can be seen just to the right of the sailor with his hand on his hip. Steamship Historical Society (#731-n)

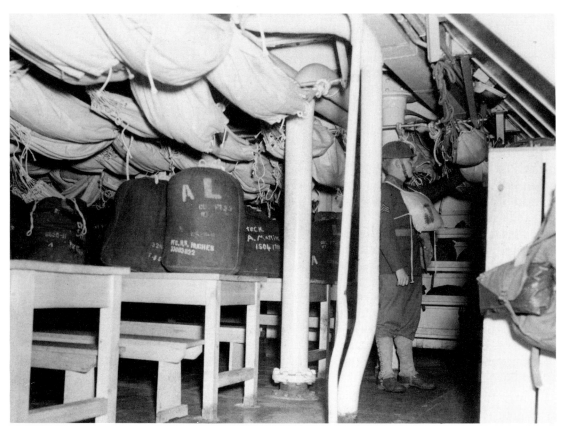

Cramped quarters aboard the Queen, *May 1942. This photo shows part of the berthing area for "C" Battery, 68th Field Artillery.*   U.S. Army Transportation Corps Museum

The first U.S. troops transported to the United Kingdom aboard the Queen Mary *left New York on May 11, 1942. One of the embarked units on that voyage was the Headquarters Staff of the U.S. 5th Army Corps, whose administrative staff is here seen at work in an improvised office.*   U.S. Army Transportation Corps Museum

was monitored aboard the liner, now safely out of reach, and Captain Bisset told the communications officer to "keep the news under your hat. Don't let the troops know we've been sunk. It might worry them." Within weeks of the incident all the members of the Axis spy ring in Rio had been arrested, and Count Di Robilant would spend several years in prison for his part in the conspiracy.

Despite heavy odds the *Queen Mary* survived the trip to Australia, and the American troops were disembarked in Sydney on March 28th. After leaving the ship the troops were taken to a huge staging area set up at Randwick Racecourse, and from there were sent on to advance bases throughout Australia and the South Pacific. The *Queen Mary,* meanwhile, used her nine-day layover in Sydney to recover from the effects of her voyage from New

York. Crewmen set to work cleaning up the refuse generated by 8,000 passengers, sections of the hull near the waterline were given another coat of gray paint, and the ship was made ready for the return voyage to New York.

As the *Queen Mary* was leaving Sydney Harbor on April sixth, bound for New York, she passed the *Queen Elizabeth.* Cunard's second superliner was just ending a voyage from San Francisco, and it was the first time the two ships had met at sea. The 8,000 American troops aboard the *Queen Elizabeth* cheered the *Queen Mary* as she passed, and the two liners saluted each other with a chorus of siren blasts. The older ship then turned south, skirted the southern end of Tasmania, and set a westerly course across the Great Australian Bight.

By May sixth the *Queen Mary* was some 600 miles southeast of New York, racing toward port at

A U.S. Army gun crew mans one of the Queen Mary's *anti-aircraft machinegun mounts during the voyage to Scotland, May 1942. This weapon is an early, water-cooled version of the famous Browning .50-caliber machinegun. Note that the G.I.s wear heavy cold-weather gear to ward off the chill of a North Atlantic spring.*

U.S. Army Transportation Corps Museum

nearly 30 knots. Shortly after dawn the bridge watch sighted a group of six lifeboats, all under sail and apparently headed for Bermuda. The liner was under strict orders not to stop in such situations, for U-boats often lurked near the scene of a sinking in order to attack any rescue vessel foolish enough to expose itself. Captain Bisset gave the lifeboats

...a wide berth, and continued zig-zagging at full speed. But I made a signal to them, slowly, with a powerful Morse lamp, stating that I would report their position and course to the Navy. This I did, and they were picked up by a U.S.N. ship the next day and taken on to Bermuda.

The lifeboats were from the Canadian transport S.S. *Lady Drake*, which had been torpedoed the day before while bound from Halifax to Bermuda. Among the survivors was the son of the *Queen Mary's* Chief Purser. The young man understood why the liner could not stop and, after reaching Bermuda, cabled his father a humorous rebuke: "Dad useless as usual, passed us by. But we made it!"

The Cunarder finally dropped anchor in New York on May 7, 1942, safely ending a 78-day voyage that had covered nearly 35,000 miles. The *Queen Mary* had navigated some of the most treacherous waters on the face of the earth, and her crew had managed to outwit the combined military and naval forces of Germany, Italy and Japan. It was a complete vindication of the faith placed in ship and crew by the liner's supporters, and the success of this first voyage with American troops erased all remaining doubts of the worth of the Cunard Queens to the Allied war effort. And, even as the *Queen Mary* was being eased alongside Pier 90 on the Hudson River, plans for her even greater participation were nearing completion in London and Washington.

Soon after the Japanese attack on Pearl Harbor both the *Queen Mary* and the *Queen Elizabeth* had come under American control. Though they remained British vessels, and their crews continued to be paid by Cunard, the liners were under the direct operational command of the United States on a sort of "reverse lend-lease" basis. During Winston Churchill's visit to Washington in the last days of 1941, General George C. Marshall had asked the Prime Minister about the possibility of modifying each ship to carry a complete American army division of some 15,000 men. General Marshall was concerned that, should either of the liners be sunk, there would be lifeboats for only about half the men. Churchill had looked Marshall in the eye and replied

...I can only tell you what WE should do. You must judge for yourselves the risks you will run. If it were a direct part of an actual operation, we should put all on board they could carry...It is for you to decide.

Before Marshall made that crucial decision, however, he decided to pay a visit to the *Queen Mary* for a firsthand look at the situation.

A few days after the liner returned from her long voyage General Marshall and members of his staff appeared at her New York pier. After touring the ship Marshall asked Harry Grattidge, the liner's Staff Captain, his opinion of the plan to carry 15,000 troops on each voyage. Grattidge had given the idea much thought, and saw only one problem —the possibility that the great weight of the men would cause the ship to list. A list of even five degrees, which might well occur if the troops gathered on one side of the liner for a farewell look at New York, would cause the *Queen Mary* to scrape the top of the Hudson Tunnel while trying to make her way toward the Atlantic. The only solution, as Staff Captain Grattidge saw it, was

...for the troops to remain wherever they are and stay perfectly still until we're over the Hudson Tunnel. When they could move again without fear of the ship listing...we could give them a green light. But from my experience of trooping that's a pretty tall order for 15,000 troops.

General Marshall, confident of his Army's discipline, assured Harry Grattidge that the soldiers would follow orders and returned to Washington to implement the new plan.

But new developments in the Middle East forced a delay in the scheduled expansion of the *Queen Mary's* trooping capacity. The German-Italian invasion of Libya at the end of March had forced London to shift large numbers of troops from Great Britain to the Mediterranean, and the United Kingdom's defenses were once again stretched thin. Allied war planners decided to reinforce the Home Islands with American troops, and the *Queen Mary* was urgently needed to transport the soldiers from New York to Scotland. She would there embark British troops, carry them on to Suez, and would be refitted to carry division-size groups upon her eventual return to New York.

The Cunarder weighed anchor on May 11th, bound for the Clyde with 9,880 U.S. troops and 875 crewmen. It was the first time in history that 10,000 persons had voyaged in one ship, and it was the first time that the *Queen Mary* carried American soldiers to the British Isles. The liner arrived in Scotland on May 16th, off-loaded her cargo of Americans and embarked 9,537 British soldiers, and set out for Suez on May 22nd. Her route took her first to Freetown, Sierra Leone, and then on to Cape Town and Simonstown in South Africa. The liner arrived in Egypt on June 22nd, disembarked her passengers, and began the return trip to the United States the following day.

The *Queen Mary* reached New York on July 21st, having stopped at both Simonstown and Rio. It had

Another U.S.-manned .50-caliber mount, this one a later air-cooled version. One wonders why a single gun seemed to require four enlisted men and an officer to operate it!   U.S. Army Transportation Corps Museum

Guns and gun-directing gear line the Queen Mary's *superstructure, May 1942. Note the 20mm cannon in the tub mount beside the liner's middle funnel.*   U.S. Army Transportation Corps Museum

been a fast and hectic trip, covering some 31,000 miles in 71 days, and the liner's crew was looking forward to a well-deserved break while the ship was undergoing her troop capacity expansion. But the urgent need to get the work finished and return the Cunarder to service kept leisure time to a minimum. All hands took part in the job, and for the next twelve days crewmen and civilian workers alike labored around the clock to complete the task. The liner's Midshipmen Bar and Observation Lounge both received their share of standee bunks, and the First Class Smoking Lounge was converted into a small but well-equipped troop hospital. Galleys and heads were upgraded yet again, still more bunks were crammed into the already packed passenger cabins, and Austin Reed's famous tailor shop in the Main Hall was turned into a stockade.

Finally, on August first, the *Queen Mary* was ready to embark on her first 15,000 troop voyage. The *entire* First U.S. Armored Division, a total of 15,125 men, boarded the liner during the night. As the Cunarder moved slowly downriver the next day the troops, most of whom had never even been on a ferryboat, were ordered to remain absolutely still. General Marshall's faith in his soldiers had not been misplaced, for none of the troops moved and the *Queen Mary* cleared the Hudson Tunnel with room to spare. Once the liner reached the open sea she began to pick up speed, and soon disappeared in the morning mists.

Five days later the people of Gourock awoke to find the *Queen Mary* riding peacefully at anchor in the Clyde. The initial 15,000 man crossing had gone off without a hitch and, upon the liner's August 16th return to New York, two more New York-Gourock-New York runs were scheduled. The first of these voyages, from September 5-19, also went well, and the dash across the U-boat infested North Atlantic soon began to seem almost routine. But on the second trip the atmosphere of normalcy vanished, and the *Queen Mary* experienced the greatest tragedy of her long career.

This fateful voyage had started out quite normally on September 27th, when the Cunarder left New York bound for the Clyde. By the morning of October second the *Queen Mary* was some forty miles north of Tory Island, off the northern coast of Ireland, and voyage WW#18E was nearing its end. Just after seven a.m. the bridge watch sighted the British cruiser HMS *Curacao*, a 4200-ton veteran of the First World War that was now used as an anti-aircraft escort ship. The cruiser's skipper, Captain Wilfred Boutwood, signalled the *Queen Mary* that he would take up station some five miles ahead, while six smaller destroyers would assume flanking positions a few miles on either side of the liner's track.

For the next five hours the convoy moved steadily toward Scotland, all hands scanning the clear skies for any sight of the German aircraft that often patrolled the area. A stiff wind from the northeast was making life difficult for the destroyers racing about in search of U-boats, but the *Queen Mary* steamed majestically on paying no heed to the choppy seas. Though the Cunarder was sailing a routine zig-zag course her great speed had allowed her to gradually overtake the slower *Curacao*, and by two o'clock in the afternoon the elderly cruiser was only a few hundred yards off the liner's starboard bow.

The *Queen Mary's* Senior First Officer, a Mr. Robinson, became increasingly concerned about the *Curacao's* proximity and ordered the helmsman to turn slightly away from the nearing cruiser. But, incredibly, the warship turned even further toward the liner, and Robinson ordered the *Queen Mary's* helm hard-a-port in a last ditch effort to avoid disaster. For a moment it looked as though the maneuver might work, for the *Curacao* seemed to veer slightly away from the liner. But, in less than an instant, the cruiser slid back across the *Queen Mary's* path and was sliced in half by the Cunarder's massive stem.

Staff Captain Harry Grattidge, resting in his cabin aft of the liner's wheelhouse, felt a convulsive jolt that he at first thought was caused by the near miss of a bomb. But when he reached the bridge, steel helmet in hand, he saw

...150 feet from the bridge on the portside, almost smothered in awesome clouds of black smoke...the fore part of a vessel going down. The Mary's *new master, Captain Gordon Illingsworth, had already rushed from the chartroom. Running to starboard I could see the afterend of the same vessel, trembling to settle beneath the waves.*

The *Queen Mary* had struck the *Curacao* eleven feet forward of her stern at an acute angle, spun the warship around, and sliced through her like an axe through cardboard.

Now, barely a minute after the collision, both sections of the *Curacao* were on fire and beginning to settle. Groups of screaming sailors were leaping into the oil-covered sea, and the American troops aboard *Queen Mary* were hurriedly throwing lifebelts and anything else that would float over the side. On the liner's bridge Captain Illingsworth ordered the Radio Officer to contact the escorting destroyers and have them move in to pick up survivors. The *Queen Mary* herself was under strick orders not to stop for *any* reason, for to do so would expose the ship and all aboard to the danger of submarine attack, and she moved on through the carnage seemingly undamaged by the collision. The destroyers were on the scene in minutes but, despite their best efforts, only 101 of the cruiser's 439 officers and men were saved.

HMS Curacao *as she appeared shortly before her fatal encounter with* Queen Mary. *Only 101 of the cruiser's 439 officers and men survived the collision.*
Imperial War Museum (#A.10645)

Damage control parties aboard the *Queen Mary* soon began to report that the liner had indeed been injured. The collision had stove in the Cunarder's stem below the waterline, and the ship's speed was forcing water through the eleven foot hole causing serious flooding in the forepeak. The *Queen Mary* , like all ships of her type, had been built with a collision bulkhead stretching from her keel to the main deck. The bulkhead would, in most instances, prevent water rushing through a buckled stem from flooding the main part of the hull. But if the entire forward section of the liner flooded, the collision bulkhead might well give way, and the weight of the water combined with the liner's speed would drive her bow beneath the waves. The ship would in effect become a massive submarine, and very few of the men aboard would survive the rapid submergence that would follow.

As soon as the extent of the damage was clear Captain Illingsworth reduced the liner's speed to ten knots. The flood of water through the crushed stem slowed somewhat, and damage control parties were able to block the hole with collision mats. A team of ship's carpenters reinforced the mats with timber shoring, portable pumps were brought in to deal with the sea water, and the *Queen Mary* was able to limp toward Scotland at 13 knots.

The liner arrived safely in Gourock on the morning of October third, and the Admiralty immediately put a complete news blackout into effect. Wartime secrecy laws would ensure that the disaster did not become public knowledge until after the duration, thereby denying the Axis an invaluable propaganda victory. Indeed, the fate of the *Curacao* was not announced until 1945, when a formal court of inquiry convened to examine the cause of the accident. After almost four years of legal maneuvering the British courts would rule that the *Queen Mary* was one third responsible for the collision, and the *Curacao* two thirds.

But the most pressing question in that winter of 1942 was whether or not the *Queen Mary* had been knocked out of the war effort by the damage she sustained in the collision with *Curacao*. Soon after the liner limped into Gourock a team of Royal Navy and Cunard Line marine engineers conducted a complete examination of the liner's crumpled stem, and decided that it was reparable. But the threat of an Axis attack on the *Queen Mary* should she remain in Scotland was extreme, to say the least, and it was decided that she would undergo repairs in Boston rather than Clydebank. The temporary collision mats and shoring timbers in her forepeak were replaced by a more substantial concrete plug for her journey west, and the Cunarder set sail for the United States on October 8th.

The *Queen Mary* entered the Boston Naval Shipyard's huge drydock on October 14th, and all outward signs of the *Curacao* disaster had disappeared by the time she re-emerged 19 days later. Though the urgent need to return the Cunarder to trooping duty left no time for the installation of an entirely new stem, the damaged area was straightened and the liner's forepeak and collision bulkhead were solidly reinforced. On November 5th a team of Coast Guard inspectors judged the vessel ready to rejoin the war effort, and she sailed that afternoon for Gourock with 10,389 American troops.

After off-loading her cargo of G.I.s in Scotland the *Queen Mary* set out December 23rd on one of the great voyages of her career. The liner had embarked 10,669 British and ANZAC troops in Gourock, and she carried them to Massawa, Ethiopia by way of Freetown, Cape Town, Aden and Suez. At Massawa she took on 9995 British soldiers for transport to Australia, and once in Freemantle she exchanged these for 8326 ANZACs bound for Scotland. The entire odyssey lasted four months and, by the time the *Queen Mary* returned to Gourock on April 22, 1943, she had carried a total of 28,990 men and voyaged almost 38,000 miles.

On May 5th the *Queen Mary* left the Clyde bound for the United States, and eight days later she entered drydock in Bayonne, New Jersey. While the Cunarder was undergoing her well-deserved overhaul a decision was being made in Washington that would completely alter the nature of her military career.

The Queen Mary's *crumpled stem after the collision with* Curacao. *Photo taken at the Boston Naval Shipyard, October 1942.* Mariner's Museum

Captain Gordon Illingsworth's official log entry concerning the Curacao *disaster, marked with an "X" in the top left of photo above. The notation was entered within minutes of the actual collision and states simply that "at ~2:12 pm, 2nd October 1942 this vessel was in collision with H.M.S. 'Curacao' in lat. 55°51'N, long 8°38'W." The entry is signed by both Capt. Illingsworth and the* Queen Mary's *assistant purser.* The Wrather Corporation

CHAPTER FOUR:
G.I. SHUTTLE

The voyages the *Queen Mary* had undertaken since the outbreak of the Second World War had been, in a very real sense, defensive moves on the part of the Allies. The Axis had been on the march in both Europe and the Pacific, and the troops carried by the liner had been desperately needed to bolster the defenses of Britain, Australia and New Zealand, and to halt the erosion of Allied strength in the Middle and Far East. There had really been no long-range Allied plan to defeat the Axis, because the United Kingdom, the Soviet Union and the United States had been much more concerned with simply staving off defeat.

But by the spring of 1943 the situation had changed substantially on all fronts. In the Pacific the United States Navy had risen from the ashes of Pearl Harbor to strike back at the Japanese, and the battles of the Coral Sea, Midway and Guadalcanal had marked the turning point in the war against the Rising Sun. American, ANZAC and British troops were already beginning to push the Japanese back and, though many hard and savage battles still lay ahead, it was clear that Japan was no longer in control of the Pacific war.

The struggle against Germany and Italy had also reached a turning point, and the myth of the Third Reich's invincibility had disappeared on the battlefields of North Africa and Soviet Russia. Great Britain's successful defense of Egypt and the Suez Canal, coupled with the Red Army's rout of the Wehrmacht at the gates of Stalingrad, combined to mark the beginning of the end for Adolph Hitler's "Thousand Year Reich." Massive around-the-clock Allied bombing raids were already turning Germany's industrial heartland into a smouldering ruin, and large fissures had begun to appear in the facade of Axis unity. In short, the Allies had faced the best that Germany, Italy and Japan could offer, and had survived. It was now time to go on the offensive.

The cornerstone of the Allied plan for the final defeat of Nazi Germany was Operation Overlord, the invasion of Hitler's "Fortress Europe." But before any such assault could be mounted the men and equipment necessary to guarantee victory had to be shipped to the battle zone, and a plan was devised for the pre-invasion buildup of American troops and materiel in the United Kingdom. Operation Bolero, as this plan was named, was intended to turn the British Isles into a massive supply depot and staging area from which the cross-Channel attack could be launched.

The speed and passenger capacity of the *Queen Mary* and *Queen Elizabeth,* both of which had been modified to carry 15,000 men at a speed of 30 knots, made them the obvious choice to bear the brunt of Operation Bolero. By operating on the New York to Britain shuttle for which they had originally been designed, the Cunard Queens would each be able to transport a full division of men to Britain in less than six days. The giant Cunarders would be joined by the *Aquitania, Mauretania, Nieuw Amsterdam* and *Ile de France,* and all six liners, known collectively as "The Monsters" because of their size, would devote themselves exclusively to Operation Bolero. Smaller ships would carry on the trooping program in the Pacific and Far East until after the defeat of Germany, at which time the Monsters could be shifted back to the war against Japan if the need arose.

The *Queen Mary* began her duty as a G.I. shuttle on the first day of June, 1943, and for the next 23 months she crossed the North Atlantic on a schedule almost as regular as that of her pre-war days. A typical voyage began with a senior officer's meeting at the Allied Combined Shipping Operations Office at 17 Battery Place in New York City. This building, which had housed the German consulate until the United States broke diplomatic relations with Hitler, was the nerve center for North Atlantic convoy operations. Here the *Queen Mary's* master conferred with representatives from the British Ministry of War Transport, the U.S. Army Transportation Corps, the New York Port of Embarkation and the U.S., Canadian and Royal navies. Details of troop loading, escort procedures and routing were decided on, and intelligence officers briefed the combined staff on the latest known dispositions of German submarines and surface raiders.

The build up of American forces in Britain in preparation for the Allied invasion of Occupied Europe was the Queen Mary's major concern once she returned to service, and she is seen here bound for Gourock with a full load of G.I.s in 1943. The photo clearly shows the American troops crowded aboard the liner, as well as the Queen's degaussing girdle and forward gun mounts.

EXCERPTS FROM LETTER ADDRESSED TO THE
BRITISH CONSULATE GENERAL, NEW YORK.

"On Monday evening last, a friend and I, on dropping in at a West Side bar fell into conversation with a group of British merchant seamen.   We had no previous acquaintance with them nor had they any knowledge of us; nevertheless, under the influence of considerable liquor and quite unprompted, these men volunteered considerable information about the operations of the ships on which they are serving, the "————" and the "————," of a military nature.   That is, they told us, unsolicited, that the "————" travels unconvoyed to ————, that she takes ———— days to make the crossing and so on. Certainly such vital information would be of interest to the enemies of the United Nations.

"Now, I am not suggesting that these lads—and they were just that, mere boys— were deliberately giving away what amounted to military secrets.   I am sure that each of them in his heart is as true to Britain and the cause of the Allies as one could wish. However, the fact remains that if this incident reported is a fair sample of the sort of thing that goes on when British sailors go ashore and drink, much information of concern to our enemies must inevitably get about.   Just how this condition could be remedied I would not presume to suggest, but, feeling that the British Government would be interested to learn of it, I have taken the liberty of addressing this letter to whom it may concern. I also made it my business to obtain the names of several of the seamen involved in the indiscreet talk reported.   If further information on this subject would be of service to you, please do not hesitate to communicate with me at the above address, either by letter or by telephone, and I shall gladly furnish such details that are in my possession as you may require."

Details of the Queen Mary's *movements remained highly classified information throughout her military career, and the ship's crew received frequent lectures on the need to maintain security. This rather straightforward flyer was handed out to the liner's crew during "Operation Bolero" as a reminder that "Loose Lips Sink Ships."*
                                                                          The Wrather Corporation

While the briefing was underway in Manhattan the *Queen Mary's* crew was busily preparing the ship for sea. On a typical shuttle voyage the ship's company consisted of 850-910 men divided into four working sections: the Deck Department; the Engine Department; the Catering and Purser's Department; and the Permanent Military Staff. Each group was assigned a pre-departure role in addition to its normal "at sea" function.

The Deck Department included the ship's Captain, Staff Captain, navigators, radio operators, quartermasters, bo'suns, general maintenance staff, ordinary and able seamen, and the liner's police and fire brigades. In port this section was responsible for the safety and security of the ship, as well as for all administrative operations and liaison with local military and civilian organizations. Once at sea, of course, the Deck Department's primary job was navigating the *Queen Mary* safely across the North Atlantic.

The smooth operation of the liner's propulsion system was the direct concern of the Engine Department. The Chief Engineer and Staff Chief Engineer headed a group of some 260 men, 105 of whom were normally rated as Engineer Officers while the remainder were boiler technicians, mechanics and able seamen. This section carried out regular engine maintenance in port, and also supervised the loading of fuel oil. The *Queen Mary* burned an average of 1,000 tons of the precious fluid every 24 hours during an Atlantic crossing, and some 8,000 tons were pumped aboard in New York prior to departure.

The Catering and Purser's Department usually totalled about 430 people, and included the Chief Purser, the ship's Chef, cooks, bakers, stewards, waiters, storekeepers and kitchen porters. This section was responsible for the care and feeding of both the ship's crew and the embarked troops at sea, and in New York supervised the loading of all provisions required for the journey. The amount of food consumed during a six day passage was awesome, and included

124,000 pounds of potatoes
53,000 pounds of butter, eggs and milk powder
31,000 pounds of sugar, coffee and tea
29,000 pounds of fresh fruit
31,000 pounds of canned fruit
18,000 pounds of jams and jellies
155,000 pounds of meat and poultry
21,000 pounds of bacon and ham
76,000 pounds of flour and cereals
4,600 pounds of cheese

In addition, the Catering and Purser's Department operated nine troop canteens aboard ship, which required the loading of 40,000 bottles of soft drinks, 5,000 cartons of cigarettes, 400 pounds of assorted candies and several crates of toilet articles. Some 6,500 tons of fresh water was pumped aboard as well, and the section was responsible for the enforcement of strict water rationing.

The Permanent Military Staff was a combination of U.S. and British officers and enlisted men, and was responsible for liaison between the embarked troops and the ship's senior staff. The group was headed by the Commandant of the Permanent Staff, and included security officers, medical officers, chaplains and Red Cross workers. The *Queen Mary's* defenses also came under this section's control, and almost four fifths of the 120 men assigned to the Permanent Staff were gunners and ordnance specialists.

The Permanent Staff's primary job in New York was, of course, the supervision of troop loading. The soldiers, brought from staging areas in New Jersey, began boarding the liner on the afternoon before her scheduled departure. Each man carried his M-1 rifle, a helmet, a canteen, cartridge belts and a full field pack, as well as two barracks bags containing complete summer and winter uniforms and the individual's personal belongings. Red Cross workers passed out coffee and donuts as the G.I.s assembled in the embarkation area, and a military band played martial music and popular dance tunes.

The troop capacity of both Queen Mary *and* Queen Elizabeth *was increased to some 15,000 men during the buildup for Operation Bolero, and special measures were instituted aboard each ship to minimize confusion caused by the crowded conditions. These signs aboard* Queen Elizabeth *direct troops to their assigned berthing areas and explain the various siren signals used in emergencies.* Imperial War Museum (#BU.6279)

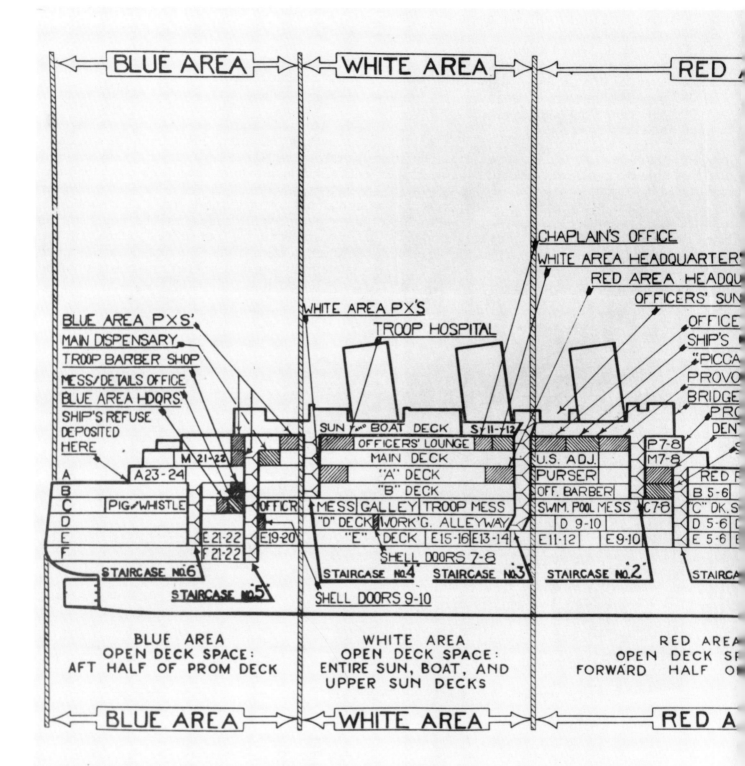

The red, white and blue accommodation plan was often a source of great confusion to troops boarding the **Queen Mary,** *and copies of explanatory diagrams like this one were passed out to help explain the system.*

The Wrather Corporation

ROOM
:US"
SHALL

A
B
C
D
E

)ECK

The *Queen Mary* had been divided into three vertical and completely segregated troop accommodation areas, designated Red, White and Blue, and each soldier boarding the liner was given a colored button corresponding to his unit's assigned area. Generally speaking, the Red area extended from the bow of the ship aft to the number three stairway, excluding the Sun Deck. The White area encompassed everything between the number three and four stairways, and included the entire Sun Deck. The remainder of the ship, from the number four stairway to the stern, was designated the Blue area. A ship's Standing Order restricted the men to their unit's area for the duration of the voyage, though individuals given work assignments outside the area in which they were quartered were allowed to move freely about the ship.

Finally, with troops, crew, fuel and provisions aboard, the *Queen Mary* was ready for sea. Departures were usually made either early in the morning or late in the evening, both to catch the maximum high tide and to screen the liner's movements from view. The Cunarder required a small flotilla of tugboats to get away from the pier and into midstream, and a pilot from the New York Port Authority then guided her slowly downriver. Once the liner cleared the Hudson Tunnel, all of her troops having been ordered to stand perfectly still at the crucial moment, the harbor pilot disembarked by launch and the *Queen Mary* made her way to the open sea.

As a precaution against Axis attack the Cunarder never followed the same route twice, and her Master did not know her exact course until after leaving port. Soon after passing the Ambrose Lightship he opened the sealed orders given him at the Shipping Office, passed the information on to the navigator, and ordered the helmsman to begin zig-zagging. A group of four of five destroyers escorted the liner for some 150 miles, and were then relieved by Navy patrol planes or blimps. The aircraft watched over the *Queen Mary* as long as their fuel allowed, then signalled GOOD LUCK and turned for home themselves. The Cunarder was then on her own until joined by her British escorts off the coast of Ireland.

The departure of the *Queen Mary's* escorts always produced a feeling of unease among the troops, for each man was well aware of the danger the ship faced on her crossing. The sight of the well-armed ships and aircraft disappearing over the horizon was a sobering one, and on each voyage the liner's Captain took this opportunity to address the troops on a subject of great importance to everyone aboard: the *Queen Mary's* survival. Though the style of the announcement differed with each Master, the tone and content never varied. Captain Gordon Illingsworth's October 1943 message, though it pertains to a specific voyage, well illustrates the theme:

Nearly every inch of free space aboard Queen Mary was jammed with standee bunks. Here the liner's swimming pool is seen jammed with tiers of folding frame beds.   Imperial War Museum (#A.25931)

Preparing meals for 15,000 hungry men was a mammoth task in itself. Here the Queen Mary's senior chef (second from left) supervises the preparation of cold meals for the troops to take away with them. The liner's catering staff also included butchers, bakers, confectioners and stewards.   Imperial War Museum (#A.25946)

Officers embarked aboard the Queen Mary *ate in the relatively tranquil atmosphere of the former Tourist Dining Room, served by members of the liner's catering staff.*   Imperial War Museum (#A.25926)

The Queen's *pre-war First Class Dining Room served as the enlisted personnel mess hall, and was always a scene of barely controlled chaos during meal times. Here Army Air Force troops queue up in the food line while other soldiers rush to finish their own meals. The wall map at upper right used a small model of the* Queen Mary *to show peacetime diners the ship's course and position.*   Imperial War Museum (#A.25923)

I call upon all officers and men to obey my orders to the letter. I have but one task. It is the job of bringing this ship safely to port, and that job, God willing, I will do. It is not important that you, numbering some 15,000, arrive safely in the Firth of Clyde, but it is important that the ship be brought safely to anchor there. Remember that. You and I are not indispensable to the successful prosecution of this war, but the ship is. You will keep in mind, therefore, that all your thoughts during the crossing will be directed toward her security. Enemy forces will be at work, and the Hun will try every device in his power to bring the "Queen" to harm. Submarines will trail us and aircraft will harass us. They have done it before and we have every reason to believe they will do it again. But the "Queen" will take care of herself. From now until the moment you debark, think in terms of the ship. Treat her gently and do not abuse her. She stands ready to do for you what she has done for thousands who have gone before. Keep her confidence and do not betray her by carelessness or misdeed. Do these things and the ship will bring us to the mouth of the Clyde on Tuesday next—so help us God.

Life for the troops embarked aboard the *Queen Mary* was regulated by the ship's Standing Orders, and by the routine Daily Orders published and distributed by the Permanent Staff. The Standing Orders covered such vital topics as emergency procedures for air attack and the outbreak of fire, as well as security precautions and the "dos and don'ts" of life at sea in wartime. The Daily Orders, on the other hand, dealt with the more mundane matters of work assignments, religious services, and the myriad of details necessary to keep 15,000 men fed and entertained for six days. The troops were informed that "ignorance of these regulations will not be accepted as an excuse in any case of breach of discipline," and were reminded that the liner's Captain held ultimate authority over all infractions committed while the ship was at sea.

But major disciplinary problems were rare during the *Queen Mary's* shuttle voyages, and the most serious infraction the Military Police usually had to contend with was the troops' almost universal disregard for the ban on gambling. Poker, blackjack and crap games sprung up almost as soon as the liner left the pier, and literally thousands of G.I.s spent the entire six day passage huddled around hastily improvised gaming tables. Other, less costly forms of entertainment could be found in the recreation halls operated by the Red Cross, and films were shown nightly in each of the three troop areas. Many of the soldiers simply chose to pass the time reading, writing letters or talking with friends, and those men of a religious nature gathered in the ship's Protestant, Catholic or Jewish chapels. Personnel inspec-

tions and twice-daily lifeboat and abandon ship drills also helped ease the monotony of the voyage, and some of the embarked units filled the time with training lectures and organized calisthenics.

Two meals were served aboard the *Queen Mary* each day, each in six staggered sittings, with breakfast available from 6:30 to 11:00 am and dinner from 3:00 to 7:30 pm. The enlisted men were fed in the former first-class dining room, and the Officer's Mess was the former tourist lounge. Meal times were usually scenes of barely controlled chaos, for each sitting was allowed only 45 minutes to enter, eat, and make room for the next group. The atmosphere was filled with cigarette smoke, the banging of mess kits and silverware, and the sound of thousands of men waiting noisily in line for their turns in the food queues. At the end of each sitting one group of soldiers would be coming in as the previous group was being ushered out the opposite end of the dining hall, and this constant flow of people contributed to an atmosphere one man later described as "a cross between a working-class cafeteria and Grand Central Station at rush hour."

The rotational system that governed meal schedules aboard the *Queen Mary* was also applied to sleeping arrangements. Only two thirds of the embarked troops could be accommodated in the liner's 12,500 standee bunks, so 2,500 men were assigned sleeping areas on the ship's decks. A regular rotation ensured that no one spent more than two nights "topside," though many of the G.I.s actually preferred it to the crowded spaces below. The standee bunks had been stacked six high in every available area, and were usually separated by only 18 inches. Most troops felt understandably claustrophobic in such cramped quarters, and believed that a man sleeping on the relatively uncluttered deck had a better chance of survival should the ship be torpedoed.

The fear of a German attack was ever-present among the troops, and the daily practice firings of the *Queen Mary's* weapons were conducted as much for morale purposes as for gunnery training. The liner's Chief Gunnery Officer controlled an impressive array of weaponry from his headquarters in the former Verandah Grill, and his U.S. and British gunners could throw up an almost impenetrable wall of fire from their machineguns, automatic 20mm and 40mm cannon, and heavy caliber high/low angle guns. These drills were always popular with the troops, both as a reassuring demonstration of the ship's ability to defend herself and as a form of welcome, if rather noisy, entertainment, and were often the high point of an otherwise boring day at sea.

But the most anxiously awaited event of every shuttle crossing was undoubtedly the arrival of the *Queen Mary's* British escorts, for it meant that the dangerous trans-Atlantic journey was nearing an

Daily shipboard weapons drills were quite popular with the troops embarked aboard the Queen Mary, *for they did much to relieve the boredom of life at sea. Here U.S. and British gunners race to their weapons as the "action stations" alarm sounds the start of yet another drill.* Imperial War Museum (#BU.6271)

Royal Navy gunners man the Queen Mary's *six-inch gun during a 1944 weapons drill.* Imperial War Museum (#A.25944)

A U.S.-manned twin 40mm cannon aboard the Queen, *1944. The two soldiers in the center of the photo are removing ammunition magazines from a special weatherproof storage bin.*
Imperial War Museum (#A.25943)

end. Seaplanes or long-range patrol bombers of the RAF's Coastal Command usually appeared while the Cunarder was still some 600 miles off the Irish coast, and were joined a few hours later by four or five Royal Navy destroyers. The escort vessels took up screening positions on the liner's flanks, taking care to stay well clear of the massive stem that had sunk the *Curacao,* and accompanied the *Queen Mary* the rest of the way to Scotland. This was always a particularly hazardous part of the passage, for a lurking U-boat would have a clear shot at the liner as she reduced speed to navigate the River Clyde approaches, and the escort ships broadened their Asdic anti-submarine search patterns accordingly.

The troops embarked aboard the *Queen Mary* normally began preparing for debarkation a few hours before the liner reached Gourock. The ship's Standing Orders specified that no unit would be allowed ashore until its particular area had been thoroughly "policed," and teams of soldiers set to work collecting the considerable amount of refuse that had accumulated during the voyage. Other troops swept and mopped the liner's decks under the supervision of the cleaning staff, and the end results of the cleanup effort were then inspected by the area commander. Once the G.I.s had passed their gear and area inspections they turned in their

lifebelts and drifted up on deck for their first sight of Scotland.

The River Clyde had become a major Allied shipping center during the first years of the war, and its drydocks, piers and shipyards were usually filled to capacity. Consequently, the *Queen Mary* normally had to navigate her way slowly upriver through a crowded assembly of merchant vessels and warships. The Cunarder had gone briefly aground during her launching in this same river, and her escorting flotilla of harbor tugs were careful to keep the heavily laden liner in the deepest part of the channel during the approach to the pier. It is a testament to the skill of the tugmen and the *Queen Mary's* crew that the huge ship always reached the docks without incident.

Once safely moored alongside her pier the *Queen Mary* set about discharging her human cargo. Gangways on A, B and D decks were normally used to off-load the troops, and the debarkation process rarely took more than 36 hours. The troops were mustered in the ship's passageways and led to the appropriate gangway by members of the liner's Permanent Staff, where other crewmen collected the colored area assignment buttons. Once on the pier the soldiers were directed to their unit assembly areas, mustered yet again, and then

Both the Queen Mary *and* Queen Elizabeth *were equipped with four 2-inch anti-aircraft rocket launchers. These experimental weapons, though of little practical value, did provide the embarked troops with a colorful show when fired during practice drills.*   Imperial War Musuem (#BU.6263)

loaded aboard waiting British Army trucks. The vehicles, forming a convoy that often stretched for miles, then wound through the streets of Gourock toward staging areas outside Glasgow. From there the Americans would be sent on to other camps throughout Britain and, ultimately, on to the battlefronts.

The *Queen Mary* usually spent only a few days in Scotland, and any shore leave granted to the crew was accordingly brief. Indeed, preparations for the return voyage to New York began almost as soon as the American troops disembarked, and the ship's company worked in round-the-clock shifts to complete necessary maintenance and repairs. Then, on the day before departure, the fuel and fresh water lines were connected to the liner's tanks, provisions and ammunition began coming aboard, and the entire shuttle cycle started again. Passengers bound for the United States boarded the ship late in the evening, the Captain received his sailing orders from the local Shipping Office, and the next morning the people of Gourock awoke to find that the Cunarder had sailed on the morning tide.

The *Queen Mary* kept up this hectic schedule from June 1943 to April 1945, and during that period sailed over 180,000 miles and carried nearly 340,000 American and Canadian servicemen to the United Kingdom. The *Queen Elizabeth* was working equally hard and, operating in concert, the two great ships transported the majority of men marshalled in Great Britain during Operation Bolero. As Sir James Bisset later explained it, the Cunarders' great value lay in the fact that

> *...each was doing work equivalent to that of ten normal troop transports. Together, they were equal to a fleet of twenty normal troop transports. That calculation takes into account their high speed, which enabled them to make more round voyages in a given time than ordinary liners could make.*

The *Queens* soldiered on through the darkest months of the Battle of the Atlantic despite the constant threat of Axis attack, and their exemplary performance earned them worldwide praise. Perhaps the greatest accolade given the ships and their crews came from Winston Churchill:

> *Built for the arts of peace and to link the Old World with the New, the* Queens *challenged the fury of Hitlerism...to defend the liberties of civilization. Vital decisions depended on their ability continuously to elude the enemy, and without their aid the day of final victory must unquestionably have been postponed. To the men who contributed to the success of our operations...the world owes a debt that it will not be easy to measure.*

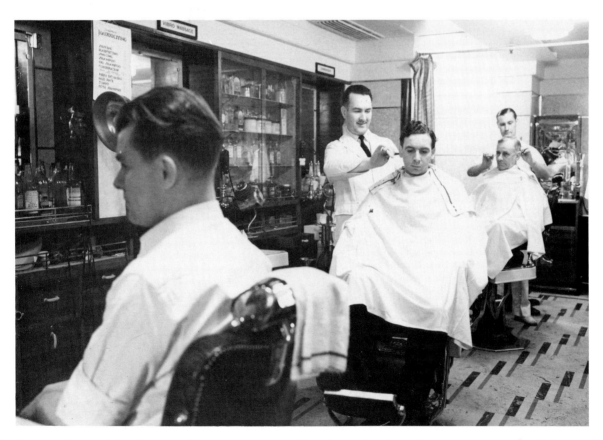

The Queen Mary *retained some of her pre-war amenities during her trooping career, one of which was the hair dressing salon shown here. Five full-time barbers offered hair cuts, vibro-massages and mud packs, though troops were not able to purchase the items displayed on the shelves.*   Imperial War Museum (#A.25930)

A pair of U.S. soldiers enjoy tea with members of the Queen Mary's *crew, 1944.*   Imperial War Museum (#A.25939)

The Queen's *pre-war Tourist Class Cocktail Bar was converted into a small troop dispensary, which was staffed by Army nurses and medical orderlies.*   Imperial War Museum (#A.25929)

While the G.I.s embarked aboard the Queen Mary *had very little to do during the five-day passage to Scotland, the ship's crew worked around the clock. Here, engineers on the control platform in the liner's after engine room closely monitor two of the* Queen's *four huge powerplants.* Imperial War Museum (#A.25947)

Many of the troops embarked aboard the Queen *spent the entire voyage in more traditional pursuits. These Army Air Force enlisted men have improvised a gaming table on the deck of their berthing area.* Imperial War Museum (#A.25928)

Daily abandon-ship drills were a fact of life aboard the Queen Mary, *and both crew and embarked passengers were required to attend. This photo shows such a drill in progress on the River Clyde prior to the* Cunarder's *return to New York.*

Another view of the abandon-ship drill. A ship's officer (center left) is adjusting an American WAC officer's life preserver.

Imperial War Museum (#A.25919)

After the Queen Mary *had unloaded her cargo of troops at Gourock she was immediately prepared for the return voyage to New York. Part of the "turn-around" process was a "clean sweepdown fore and aft," provided here by some of the 125 cleaning women assigned to the ship's Gourock-based maintenance crew.*

Imperial War Museum (#A.25949)

The most eagerly awaited sight on any shuttle voyage: the arrival of an RAF Coastal Command Catalina patrol plane off the coast of Ireland means the passage is nearly over. The last day of a shuttle crossing was always the most dangerous, for German aircraft and patrol boats often tried to intercept the Queen Mary as she reduced speed to navigate the River Clyde approaches. Note that the 20mm cannon lining the ship's superstructure have been swung skyward, as their crews carefully scan the horizon for any sign of trouble.

Imperial War Museum (#A.18953)

CHAPTER FIVE:
PRISONERS, PATIENTS AND V.I.P.S

The primary reason for the *Queen Mary's* original induction into military service had, of course, been her tremendous value as a troop transport. But the same qualities that made her indispensable in the trooping role—her size, speed and ability to safely navigate routes unsuitable for smaller vessels—made her the ideal choice for a variety of other vital tasks as well.

One of the first subsidiary duties assigned to the *Queen* after her requisitioning was that of transporting Axis prisoners of war from the Mediterranean and Middle Eastern battle zones to rear area detention centers. Since guarding and caring for large numbers of captured German and Italian soldiers would put a considerable strain on the Home Island's already overtaxed resources, His Majesty's Government decided to establish permanent POW camps in South Africa and Australia. The *Queen Mary,* already employed on the Indian Ocean run and capable of carrying far more prisoners than any other ship, was chosen to bear the brunt of the POW relocation program in addition to her normal trooping duties.

But before the Cunarder could begin this new task she required some rather special alterations. Those areas of the ship in which the prisoners would be housed were cleared of all fittings that could be used as weapons, additional locks were installed on stateroom and passageway doors, and the prisoners' dining and exercise areas were enclosed by barbed-wire barricades. Sandbagged machine gun emplacements were erected at strategic points to discourage any attempt at a concerted breakout, and a system of alarm bells ensured that Allied guards could summon help quickly should the need arise.

Thus prepared, the *Queen Mary* embarked her first load of Axis POWs at Suez in the spring of 1941. For the next year the liner routinely carried an average of 2,000 captured German and Italian troops on her return voyages to Australia from the Middle East. The prisoners, most of whom were former members of General Erwin Rommel's famed Afrika Korps, were surpisingly docile and normally caused little trouble for their captors beyond minor acts of passive resistance. Captain James Bisset later recalled a typical example of the low-key battle of wills that went on constantly between the prisoners and their guards. In June of 1942 a group of German POWs were

> *...scrawling anti-British slogans on the bulk-heads of their cabins. When these were found, the occupants had to clean them off, and were then put into the "brig" on a bread-and-water diet for a few days. Next, six men in one of the cabins decided to be sarcastic, and wrote "Rule Britannia" in large letters on the bulkhead. They too were punished, just to show that we played no favorites!*

Soon after America entered the war the *Queen Mary* began carrying POWs to New York, and during each of her stops at that port from January 1942 onward the liner off-loaded several thousand prisoners bound for detention camps in Canada and the United States. The number of captured troops evacuated to North America increased steadily as the Allies pushed the Axis back in North Africa and the Mediterranean, and by December 1943 over 170,000 German and Italian soldiers were being held in the U.S. alone. The Allied advance across Europe that followed the June 1944 Normandy invasion bagged still more prisoners, and in the peak month of September 1944 over 55,000 German troops were sent to the United States from clearing stations in France and Great Britain. Many of these unwilling guests got their first glimpse of America through the *Queen Mary's* portholes, for by the end of 1944 the Cunarder was carrying an average of 5,000 POWs to New York on the return leg of each shuttle crossing to Scotland.

But though the D-Day landings marked the beginning of the end for Adolph Hitler's "Thousand Year Reich," the German Army was by no means ready to surrender en masse and many hard and costly battles still lay ahead for the Allies. The invasion itself had been fiercely resisted by the Wehrmacht, and the advancing British, American and Canadian forces suffered increasingly heavy casualties as they pushed toward the Rhine. A well-organized medical evacuation system ensured that the vast majority of these wounded troops were quickly transferred from frontline aid stations to better-equipped facilities in the United Kingdom. But a chronic shortage of hospital and medical transport ships hindered the final evacuation of American troops to the United States, and Britain's hospitals were soon filled to capacity as casualties continued to pour in from the Continent. It was a potentially critical problem, and the U.S. Office of the Surgeon General and the Army's Transportation Corps immediately set out to speed the repatriation process and thus alleviate the overcrowding in the British Isles.

In the months following the invasion of France nearly every vessel capable of carrying passengers was pressed into medical service. Liberty ships designed to carry bulk cargo were modified to transport 500 litter and ambulatory patients. The few hospital ships available in the European Theater were reconfigured to house twice their normal number of casualties, and troop transports returning to the United States were detailed to carry "as many injured personnel as might be physically possible." But the Transportation Corps and Surgeon General's Office were at first reluctant to employ the Cunard Queens on large-scale medical evacuation duty even though, at first glance, the liners seemed ideally suited to the task. Each ship had been built with a small but well-equipped hospital, and had been furnished with

One of the first subsidiary tasks assigned to both the Queen Mary and Queen Elizabeth was that of transporting Axis prisoners-of-war from North Africa to detention centers in South Africa and Australia. Here a group of German POWs, former members of General Erwin Rommel's famed Afrika Korps, assemble in Suez prior to boarding ship, July 1942.   Imperial War Museum (#E.14712)

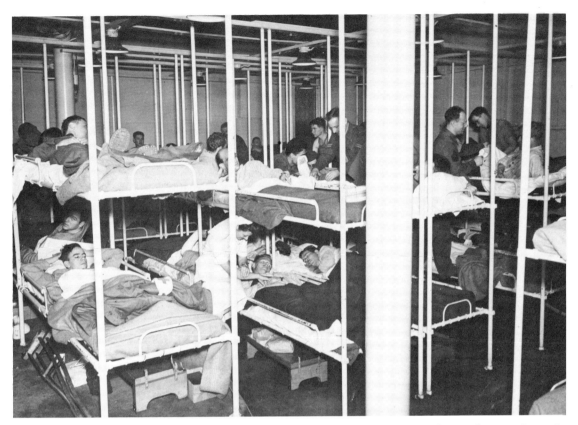

The Queen Mary's *pre-war Main Ballroom fitted out as a troop hospital. Both of Cunard's superliners transported increasing numbers of American and Canadian wounded to New York following the Allied invasion of Occupied Europe.*   Imperial War Museum (#A.25927)

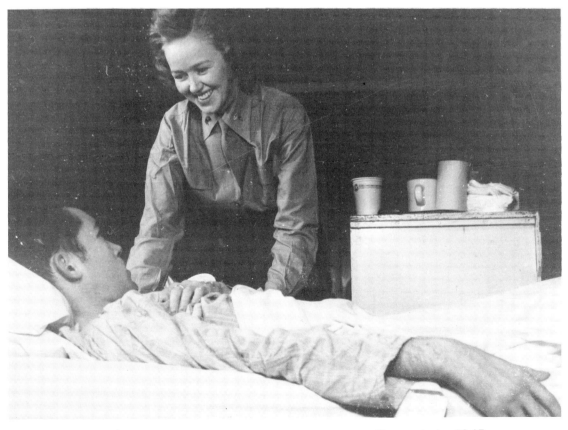

Tender loving care, American-style. A U.S. Army nurse jokes with one of her patients, 1945.
Imperial War Museum (#BU.6253)

several troop dispensaries prior to entering military service. The Cunarders appeared capable of carrying far more casualties than the other vessels then in use, and each would be able to make two trips to New York in the same time a lesser ship would require for a single passage.

But, despite their size, speed, and apparent suitability, neither of the *Queens* was actually able to handle any significant number of seriously wounded soldiers. The medical facilities aboard the *Queen Mary,* for example, had always been quite sufficient for dealing with seasickness, broken bones or the occasional minor operation—the normal complaints encountered during a trooping voyage— but the liner could supply beds for fewer than 50 seriously ill or injured persons. No provision had been made for transporting mental patients or troops requiring intensive care or isolation, simply because the *Queen Mary's* primary military task had always been that of carrying perfectly healthy men and more extensive medical facilities had not been necessary. And, though both the *Queens* could certainly be modified for medical evacuation work, the Transportation Corps estimated that the conversion would take several weeks and thus interfere with the liners' most important mission, that of transporting desperately needed *healthy* troops to the battle zones.

But by the fall of 1944 the need for medical evacuation ships had become so acute that the Cunard *Queens* were pressed into service despite the problems involved. Both ships were surveyed in

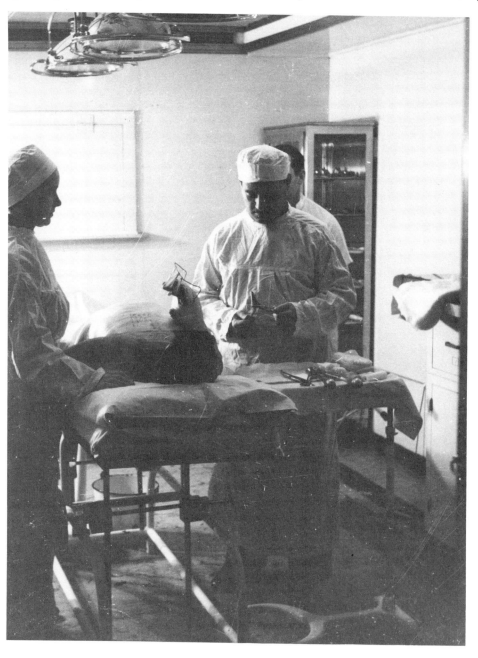

Both of the Queens *were equipped with small but well-appointed surgical suites. Here a U.S. Army surgeon treats a badly wounded G.I. in the* Queen Elizabeth's *operating theater.*   Imperial War Museum (#BU.6282)

New York during the first days of October and, after hurried negotiations between the British Ministry of War Transport, the Army Transportation Corps and the U.S. Surgeon General's Office, each liner was judged capable of carrying 1,000 litter and 700 ambulatory patients. On the *Queen Mary* this necessitated the installation of 1,084 single and double tier hospital beds in place of the standee bunks on the Main, Promenade and "A" decks, and the addition of a small but well-equipped laboratory adjacent to the Promenade deck. Several large staterooms were turned into exercise and recreation areas, and separate kitchens were set up in cabins on the Main deck to prepare the special foods some patients would require. In order to deal with the increased work load the liner's permanent British-American medical staff was increased from five officers and 30 other ranks to ten medical officers, 30 nurses, and 250 orderlies and attendants.

Contrary to original estimates the entire conversion process took less than ten days, and the *Queen Mary* was able to sail for Scotland with 11,891 troops on October 12th. After unloading the G.I.s at Gourock the liner took on 1,600 patients and began the return voyage to New York on October 22nd. She kept up this routine for the next four months, carrying replacements to Great Britain and returning with an average of 1,500 casualties in addition to her usual cargo of prisoners of war. But by January 1945 the imminent end of the war in Europe made further large-scale POW shipments to North America unnecessary, and the *Queen Mary's* patient capacity was increased by converting former prisoner confinement areas into hospital wards. For the remainder of her shuttle service the liner was thus able to carry 2,000 litter and 1,000 ambulatory casualties on each return voyage to New York.

During her military career the *Queen Mary* was often called upon to carry "Very Important Passengers" in addition to her normal complement of troops, patients and prisoners. Despite her war paint and weaponry she remained the "stateliest ship afloat" and, though her accommodations were

A church service for American walking wounded, April 1945.

Imperial War Museum (#BU.6292)

The Queen Mary, *with "Colonel Warden" aboard, steams toward Halifax, 1943.*

not quite up to Cunard's exacting pre-war standards, the statesmen, diplomats, newsmen, entertainers and military leaders who voyaged aboard her could hardly complain. The liner was usually the fastest available form of transportation between the far-flung Allied nations, and she was undoubtedly more comfortable and vastly safer than the vulnerable transport aircraft and slow-moving convoy vessels that were the only other link between Europe, America, Australia and the Far East.

Though the *Queen Mary* carried such well-known personalities as Bob Hope, Katherine Cornell, and Sir Thomas Beecham, among others, her most important wartime passenger was undoubtedly the Right Honorable Winston S. Churchill. The great British Prime Minister made three roundtrip Atlantic crossings aboard the liner, travelling via New York to the May 1943 Trident Conference in Washington and by way of Halifax, Nova Scotia, to the August 1943 Quadrant and September 1944 Octagon Conferences in Quebec. Mr. Churchill was accompanied on these voyages by such military and civilian leaders as Lord Leathers, the Minister of War Transport; Field Marshal Wavell, Commander-in-Chief in India; Lord Louis Mountbatten, Supreme Allied Commander in South East Asia; General Orde Wingate, the leader of the famous Chindit guerillas in Burma; and, on one occasion, the entire Imperial General Staff. In addition, the Prime Minister's entourage always included aides, communications personnel, cypher clerks, secretaries and a large bodyguard of Royal Marine commandoes.

The Axis would obviously have gone to even greater lengths to locate and destroy the *Queen Mary* had Churchill's presence aboard become known, so prior to each of the Prime Minister's voyages on the liner British Intelligence concocted and circulated elaborate cover stories to conceal the "special party's" identity. Rumors were planted among the Clydebank dockworkers that very important POWs were being transferred to camps in Canada, that exiled European monarchs were travelling to America, or that the liner was transporting several hundred patients suffering from an undisclosed but "highly contagious" disease. The ship always embarked a normal load of prisoners and bona fide casualties to allay suspicion, and the passenger list mentioned only a "Colonel Warden" or simply "239 and party." Churchill and his staff always boarded the Cunarder at Gourock under cover of darkness, and no one from the "special party" was allowed on deck until after the *Queen* cleared the Firth of Clyde. Once in open water the liner would set out across the Atlantic at flank speed, accompanied the entire way by a strong escort of Royal Navy cruisers and destroyers.

On each voyage aboard the *Queen Mary* Prime Minister Churchill and his group were quartered in Main deck staterooms especially refurbished for the occasion. Furniture and fittings brought out of storage in Cunard's warehouses replaced the usual drab military decor, baskets of fruit and candy stood on well-polished sideboards, and vases of fresh flowers filled each cabin. The "special party" dined on such delicacies as Macaroni Bolognaise, Navarin of Lamb and Corned Ox Tongue, and red-jacketed Royal Marine aides offered cigars and after dinner mints from silver trays bearing the Prime Minister's family coat of arms.

But the atmosphere of peacetime luxury was deceiving, for Churchill firmly believed in making the most of every day at sea. There were plans to be made for the invasion, details of the Allied aerial offensive against Germany to be worked out, and a hundred other agenda items that had to be dealt with before the *Queen Mary* reached her destination. Several larger cabins adjoining the Main deck had been converted into working spaces, and the Prime Minister and his staff maintained the same grueling schedule afloat as they did ashore. General Sir Hastings Ismay, Churchill's Chief of Staff, later recalled that

WREN cypher experts attached to Prime Minister Churchill's staff at work in the Queen Mary's *communications office.* Imperial War Museum (#A.25937)

The Queen Mary *was a most convenient and comfortable workshop. We were all under one roof, and each had our own offices. There were ample conference rooms, and the production and circulation of papers went forward with the same methodical precision as in London. We received the usual stream of telegrams, and the Prime Minister's Map Room...was kept as up to date as its counterpart in Great George Street.*

All this activity generated quite a bit of message traffic and, because the liner was required to observe radio silence, special arrangements were made for the transmission of outgoing signals. As General Ismay later remembered,

These were signalled by visual means to attendant destroyers which, after placing sufficient distance between themselves and us to avoid giving away our position, passed them on to London.

There was, as Ismay expressed it, "never a dull moment" for the members of Churchill's harried staff. The Prime Minister himself later acknowledged that "from the time we got on board our work went on ceaselessly," and the passageways of the sealed-off "special party" area echoed around the clock with the sound of typewriters and code machines. Indeed, the only opportunity Churchill and most of his group had to get out on deck came during the liner's mandatory lifeboat drills. But while most of his subordinates saw the exercise as a welcome respite from the crushing workload, the Prime Minister characteristically put the time to more pragmatic use. On his first voyage aboard the *Queen* Churchill had insisted his lifeboat be equipped with a .50 caliber Browning machinegun so that he might "actively resist capture" should the liner be sunk. On each Atlantic crossing he therefore spent the lifeboat drill periods reacquainting himself with the weapon's operation and maintenance. The Prime Minister was never required to put his gunnery skills to the test, however, for the Cunarder and her crew never failed to safely deliver the "Special Party" to its final destination.

Though the *Queen Mary* was admirably suited for duty as a patient, prisoner and VIP transport, her primary wartime task remained that of ferrying American troops to Great Britain. But by early April 1945 Allied forces were pouring into Germany from all sides, and the Reich's imminent collapse made further trooping voyages unnecessary. The *Queen's* shuttle service to Scotland was thus suspended following her April 4th arrival in New York from Gourock, and she went into drydock at Bayonne on April 18th. Thirteen days later Adolph Hitler killed himself in his Berlin bunker, and on May 7th the unconditional surrender of Nazi Germany ended the Second World War in Europe. It was an event the world had anxiously awaited for six long and terrible years, and one that marked the beginning of yet another phase in the military career of His Majesty's Transport *Queen Mary.*

The Queen Mary *docked at Halifax prior to returning Mr. Churchill and his staff to Britain, 1943.*

Public Archives of Canada (#REA 253-72)

Mr. Churchill flashes the "V for Victory" sign to cheering troops as he and Mrs. Churchill leave the Queen Mary *at Gourock, September 1944.*
Imperial War Museum (#H.40334)

The Prime Minister and Captain Bisset pose for photographers aboard the Queen Mary, *September 1944. Mrs. Churchill stands to the Prime Minister's right.*
Imperial War Museum (#H.40328)

CHAPTER SIX: PEACE AND REPATRIATION

In the weeks following Germany's surrender the nations of the Allied world uttered a collective sigh of relief and gave full vent to the euphoria of victory. Millions of people from Suez to Stalingrad, from London to Los Angeles, took to the streets to celebrate the death of Nazism, and the long-dimmed lights flickered back to brilliant life as Europe began digging itself out of the rubble caused by six long years of war. But the festive atmosphere was tempered by the knowledge that Allied troops were still fighting and dying in the Pacific and Far East, and that many hard and desperate battles still lay ahead in the struggle against the Rising Sun. Though badly mauled, Japan was by no means beaten, and Allied war planners were predicting that one *million* troops would be lost in the expected invasion of the Japanese home Islands. It was a sobering thought, indeed.

The first step in the final assault against Japan was the redeployment of several hundred thousand Allied troops from Europe to the Pacific Theater. The transportation plan drawn up by the Combined Allied Command called for Commonwealth forces to be shipped directly to Australia and India from the United Kingdom and the Middle East, while the majority of American units in Europe would reorganize and re-equip in the United States before deploying to the Pacific from west coast ports. The *Queen Mary*, *Queen Elizabeth* and *Aquitania* were chosen to bear the brunt of this repatriation program for obvious reasons: they were already operating on the UK-US shuttle, they were fully equipped to handle large numbers of American troops, and their speed and passenger capacity would allow them to move the greatest number of men to the United States in the shortest possible time.

The *Queen Mary* began this latest military task on the morning of June 5, 1945, when she set sail from New York bound for Gourock. Though her course took her over the same route she had been travelling for the past two years, this voyage was vastly different from her previous wartime crossings. Peacetime conditions once again prevailed on the North Atlantic, and for the first time since 1939 the great liner was able to sail a straight course without the need to zig-zag. No U-boats lay in wait for her, no surface raiders stalked her, and the only aircraft overhead were friends. The Cunarder sped on with every light blazing brightly, and arrived at Gourock on June 10th to an ecstatic welcome.

But if the liner was warmly received in Scotland, her return to New York on June 20th can only be described as tumultuous. The 14,777 American troops she had embarked in Gourock five days earlier were the first to to returned to the United States as brigaded units, and New York's enthusiastic welcome knew no bounds. Captain James Bisset later recalled that the G.I.s returned the city's greeting with equal fervor, for as the *Queen Mary* moved slowly upstream just after noon the troops

swarmed onto the upper decks, excitedly cheering at their first view for many a day of the Statue of Liberty and of "Little Old New York." Blimps and helicopters flew low overhead, with loudspeakers blaring out the latest songs and messages of "Welcome Home!" Harbour craft steamed alongside, with flags flying, bands playing, and crowded with thousands of cheering people. Every ship in the harbour blew three long blasts of welcome as we passed, and the Queen Mary's deep-toned steam whistle... responded with an almost continuous series of blasts that made a deafening roar. The ship was gaily decorated with flags, as also was the Cunard White Star Pier, and flags flew everywhere on the masts of the skyscrapers, from the windows of which people were leaning out, waving flags and throwing down showers of paper.

We docked at 3:10 p.m., and the troops began disembarking immediately, while bands played and the crowds cheered, laughed and wept with joy at the heroes' homecoming.

The welcome accorded the *Queen Mary* in New York was no less boisterous on her next three arrivals from Scotland, and by mid-August 1945

31,955 returning American soldiers had witnessed the same scene from the liner's decks. But these G.I.s were not the only ones to receive a warm welcome home, for the British men, women and children the Cunarder carried to the United Kingdom on her eastbound passages got the same sort of reception at Gourock. The majority of these returning Britons had been evacuated to the United States and Canada during the first months of the war and had not seen family, friends or homeland for more than five years. The people of the Clyde turned out in force to welcome them home, and though the bands, flags and crowds on the Gourock piers could not compete in numbers with those in New York, the greeting was no less joyous.

On August 11th the *Queen Mary* arrived at Southhampton for the first time since 1939. The huge port had been heavily damaged by German air attacks, and wreckage still littered the area as the liner moved slowly up the channel toward her pier. Nothing could dampen the enthusiasm of the crowds waiting to meet the ship, however, and she was treated to yet another rousing homecoming. But this welcome was even more intense than those in New York and Gourock, for the scent of a final Allied victory was heavy in the air. The world had been abruptly ushered into the Atomic Age while the *Queen* was still at sea—Hiroshima had been obliterated on August 6th and Nagasaki had vanished beneath an awesome mushroom cloud three days later—and rumours of an imminent Japanese capitulation had been circulating in Britain for several days. On August 14th, as the Cunarder was preparing to embark 15,000 American troops bound for New York, the rumours became fact. Emperor Hirohito, speaking to his subjects by radio for the first time, announced Japan's unconditional surrender to the Allied Powers. After six

The end of the war in Europe brought the Queen Mary's *New York-to-Gourock trooping shuttle to a close, and she is seen here in New York in April 1945, awaiting the next phase of her military career. Note that the liner's guns and degaussing girdle have not yet been removed.* U.S. Army Transportation Corps Museum

Homeward bound at last! Troops of the U.S. 30th Division wave goodbye to Europe as the Queen Mary
leaves Southampton for New York, 1945.

U.S. Army Historical Center

-61-

long and bitter years, and a worldwide toll of at least ten *million* dead, the Second World War had at last come to an end.

In America the Japanese collapse sparked an immediate and vocal public demand for the rapid repatriation of all overseas U.S. forces not absolutely required for occupation duty. The Truman Administration quite understandably reacted to the increasing pressure by assigning nearly every possible vessel to repatriation work. Some 178 Army and Navy assault transports, 111 surface combatants, 8 hospital ships and dozens of converted cargo transports, cruise ships and captured enemy freighters were eventually pressed into service in what soon became the largest sealift operation in history. The Cunard *Queens* were of course called upon to play a major role in the redeployment effort and, working in concert with the *Aquitania*, formed the backbone of the transport program in the Atlantic Theater. By maintaining a regular Southampton–New York shuttle service the three Cunarders by themselves transported nearly a quarter of the 500,000 U.S. troops returned to America by October 1945.

The success of the redeployment program soon mollified American public opinion but, ironically, fuelled a similar controversy then raging in the United Kingdom. Prime Minister Clement Attlee's government was being accused by the British press of subordinating the best interests of the United Kingdom to those of the United States. The *Queen Mary, Queen Elizabeth* and *Aquitania* had been loaned to the American government after Germany's surrender solely to speed the redeployment of European-based G.I.s to the Pacific Theater. But Tokyo's unexpectedly rapid capitulation had terminated that agreement in August, and many Britons were openly wondering why the ships were still being used to repatriate American rather than British troops. As Prime Minister Attlee expressed it in a cable to President Truman in early October 1945:

> While so many of our troops overseas are awaiting repatriation after nearly six years of war and separation from their families, I cannot continue to justify to the British public the use of our three biggest ships in the American service.

Though Attlee was reluctant to request the return of the three liners he did urge President Truman to "provide us in the immediate future with an equivalent lift." Truman well understood the Prime Minister's position, and ordered the Army Transportation Corps to solve the problem through negotiations with representatives of the Ministry of War Transport. The two agencies quickly reached a mutually acceptable agreement, and on October 12th announced that the *Queen Elizabeth* and the *Aquitania* would return "immediately" to British service while the *Queen Mary* would continue to transport American personnel "for the present."

The United States also agreed to allocate ten Victory ships and two smaller vessels to the transportation of British troops, in partial compensation for the continued American use of the *Queen Mary.*

The plan worked out by the Transportation Corps and the Ministry of War Transport was perfectly acceptable to both the American and British governments, but was not quite as popular in other quarters. Several major U.S. newspapers saw the return of the *Queen Elizabeth* and the *Aquitania* as a serious blow to the American troop repatriation program, and made their displeasure with the plan known in front page stories. On October 17th, for example, the *New York Times* gave extensive coverage to a report from U.S. Army Headquarters in Paris which estimated the return of the ships would

> ...retard the redeployment program by one month. It was pointed out that transportation would have to be provided for 221,900 men by Jan. 1, 1946, if the program were to operate on schedule, but that the withdrawal of (the) British vessels would not permit that goal to be reached before the end of January.

The Times need not have worried, however, for the transport program was actually doing quite well despite the loss of the two Cunarders. The return of the *Queen Elizabeth* and the *Aquitania* to British control had prompted a herculean effort on the part of the *Queen Mary* and the remaining U.S. ships assigned to the Atlantic Theater, and the small armada was managing to keep pace with the demands of the troop repatriation schedule. Indeed, by mid-January 1946 the bulk of American forces had been repatriated from Europe—some 46,000 troops aboard the *Queen Mary* alone—and the War Department was able to term the Atlantic Theater redevelopment progam "essentially completed." Now only one important task remained for the *Queen* and her crew before their own demobilization.

Many Americans had married foreign-born women while stationed overseas during the Second World War, and during 1944 and 1945 public demand steadily increased for the transportation of these "war brides" and their children to the United States. Such a program remained a low priority until after the repatriation of American forces, but once that goal was achieved the Transportation Corps moved quickly to implement "Operation Diaper." In January 1946 the War Department announced that 60,000 dependents from Europe and 6,000 from New Zealand and Australia would be brought to America by the following June. Some 30 ships were assigned to the project, and the British government agreed that the *Queen Mary* should remain in U.S. service at least until May 1946 to serve as the nucleus of the Atlantic Theater dependent transport program.

But the liner would require extensive modifica-

American troops pass the time in a traditional way, en route for New York aboard the Queen, *1945.*

Imperial War Museum (#BU.6291)

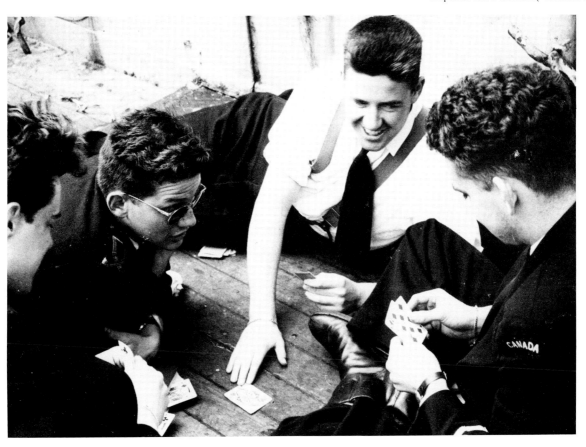

Returning Canadian troops were not averse to a bit of sport either!

Imperial War Museum (#BY.6290)

The Queen Mary *steams into New York Harbor, April 1945, her decks crowded with G.I.s eager for a glimpse of the city's famous skyline.*
U.S. Army Transportation Corps Museum

tions before she could take her place as the flagship of America's Atlantic "bride and baby" fleet, and on January 14th she entered Southampton's huge King George V graving dock to undergo yet another in her long series of conversions. For the next sixteen days workmen labored around the clock to prepare the *Queen Mary* for her new role, with the greatest attention given to stripping her of the military hardware accumulated during six years of war. Tons of plate steel armor that had protected the liner's vital areas were removed, as were the splinter shields over her bridge windows and the hundreds of sandbags stacked throughout the ship. Those barbed-wire barricades that remained from her POW voyages were dismantled and carted away, and the thousands of standee bunks that filled every available space were broken down and laid in seemingly endless rows on the Southampton docks.

Most of the *Queen Mary's* armament had been removed in New York the previous June, but the few weapons that remained were now crated up and dispatched to local military armories. The circular steel baseplates that had once supported the Cunarder's three- and six-inch guns were unbolted from the deck and winched ashore, and the empty gun tubs lining her superstructure were cut up for scrap. But Cunard and the Royal Navy agreed that the *Queen's* deguassing girdle should remain in place, at least for the time being, for the North Atlantic was still littered with dozens of drifting German magnetic mines sown during the last months of the war.

Once the *Queen Mary* had been sufficiently demilitarized the Southampton work crews set about making the special interior modifications the liner would require in her new role. On each dependent voyage the Cunarder would carry some 1,200 adult passengers in addition to a large staff of Red Cross workers, WACs, doctors, nurses and stewardesses, and the Transportation Corps directed that conditions aboard ship should be as close to prewar standards as possible. Each of the liner's staterooms was thus equipped with six relatively comfortable beds, rather than the 12 to 16 standee bunks that had been common during the *Queen's* trooping voyages, and those cabins slated to house expectant mothers were equipped with call bells connected to the ship's hospital. The Cunarder had transported most of her own off-loaded furniture from New York warehouses to Southampton during her later wartime crossings, and now these furnishings once again began to appear throughout the ship. Finally, the former troop messhalls were reconverted into dining areas, complete with starched tablecloths, and several of the shops in the Main deck arcade were reopened.

The *Queen Mary's* stay at Southampton also included a general overhaul, and though there wasn't time for every piece of machinery to be inspected the liner's engineers did what they could to prepare the ship for six more months of strenuous activity. The *Queen's* boilers, engines and steering gear were examined and worn or defective parts replaced, and maintenance crews scraped as much of the hull as possible. Teams of seamen cleaned or replaced several hundred rusted fittings, holy-stoned the decks, and in general gave the liner a "clean sweep fore and aft." One of the more important cleaning tasks, from Cunard's point of view, was the removal of vast amounts of graffiti that had accumulated throughout the ship during the war years. The troops, prisoners and casualties that had been the liner's main passengers for the preceding six years had, like all soldiers, passed the time inscribing names, dates, verse and certain rather explicit romantic propositions on nearly every exposed surface. Cunard did not wish to embarrass the soon-to-be-embarked women and children with this doggerel, and teams of sailors were thus issued paint and brushes and put to work blotting out the unsightly and sometimes offensive scribblings. The troops had defaced most of the ship's teak railings as well, and temporary wooden inserts were installed in place of the carved-up sections pending a more permanent refurbishment during the liner's post-demobilization refit.*

On January 30, 1946 His Majesty's Transport *Queen Mary* was judged mechanically and cosmetically ready to join the "bride and baby fleet." She left for New York six days later with 2,451 women and children aboard, and arrived in America on February 10th to a rousing welcome. A week later she was on her way back to Southampton with 1,720 assorted passengers, and for the next three months her trans-Atlantic routine hardly varied. Upon each return to Southampton from the United States the *Queen* would refuel and reprovision at the Cunard pier while her cargo of dependents was being trucked in from assembly areas in the nearby cities of Tidworth and Bournemouth. The U.S. Army's 14th Major Port detachment would clear the women and children through immigration and customs formalities as quickly as possible, then allow them to board the liner while their relatives waved tearful goodbyes from the crowded piers.

---

*Several of these railing sections later ended up as exhibits in various maritime and military museums, most notably the Army Transportation Corps Museum at Fort Eustis, Virginia.

A returning soldier's favorite greeting graces Cunard's New York pier, April 1945.

The Cunard Line, via the Wrather Corporation

ARMY SERVICE FORCES
TRANSPORTATION CORPS
ARMY OF THE UNITED STATES
NEW YORK PORT OF EMBARKATION

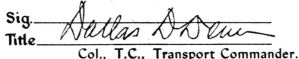

_____

_____

_____

returned to the **UNITED STATES** on the ship "QUEEN MARY" (Cunard White Star) which sailed from Southampton, England on 11th October, 1945

Sig. _____

Title _____

Col., T.C., Transport Commander.

RPB—6-20-45—500M

After the cessation of hostilities the U.S. Army Transportation Corps provided commemorative certificates to every soldier returning to the U.S. through the N.Y.P.O.E. Certificates like the one above were issued to troops embarked on voyage #WW 55 W, which arrived in New York on 16 October 1945. Wrather Corporation

The journey from Southampton to New York normally took just under five days, and the war brides passed the time at sea by attending a continual round of lectures, classes and social gatherings. The *Queen Mary's* medical staff offered instruction in child care and nutrition, and American Red Cross volunteers hosted well-attended lectures on life in the United States. There were also cooking and sewing classes, English language lessons and afternoon teas, and the liner's small library provided interested passengers with books on American history and politics. In the evenings there were films, bingo games and impromptu concerts, as well as dancing lessons held in the First Class dining room.

While their mothers were thus engaged the children aboard the *Queen Mary* amused themselves in the ship's nursery and playrooms. The Cunarder's carpenters had constructed hobby horses and dollhouses for the younger dependents, and the older children were treated to tours of the liner's engine rooms and working spaces. There were surprisingly few problems with the children, aside from an occasional case of the measles or flu,

and the ship's company unanimously agreed that the youngsters were far less troublesome passengers than most of their American fathers had been during the *Queen's* trooping career.

The United States and Great Britain had agreed that the *Queen Mary* would be transferred to the Canadian dependent transport program no later than May 1, 1946, and nine days before that deadline the liner arrived in New York with her final load of U.S.-bound women and children. During her service with the American "bride and baby fleet" the Cunarder had made five roundtrip Atlantic crossings, steamed more than 31,800 miles and carried over 12,200 dependents to new lives in the United States. The *Queen* managed to maintain her demanding schedule despite fuel shortages in Britain, unusually rough North Atlantic seas and repeated tugboat strikes in New York, and succeeded in safely transporting nearly 25 percent of all service dependents brought from Europe in the year following the end of World War II. It was indeed an outstanding performance, but one that the liner would herself soon surpass.

-67-

While the Queen Mary *was busy transporting war brides and returning U.S. and Canadian troops, the Port of Southampton was being readied for its debut as the world's ultimate ocean terminal. Here a crew of workmen are busy repairing one of the port's bomb-damaged piers as the still-camouflaged* Queen Mary *is eased away from the dock by a flotilla of harbor tugs. The Cunarder* Aquitania, *herself a veteran of numerous trooping voyages, stands securely moored to the pier at center right.* Southampton City Council, via the Wrather Corporation

On May 5th the *Queen Mary* left Southampton bound for Halifax, Nova Scotia. On this first Canadian dependent voyage the liner carried 2,495 war brides and children, and she made the 2,735 mile passage in just four days and two hours. She and her passengers were warmly received in Halifax, though the flotilla of small boats, tugs and car ferries that rushed to greet the huge ship actually delayed her mooring for nearly two hours! Finally, just after four p.m., the Cunarder made fast to her pier and began disembarking her precious human cargo. The huge crowd gathered on the docks broke into cheers as the first dependents moved slowly down the liner's four portside gangways, a military band struck up the national anthem, and any hope of an orderly debarkation disappeared as thousands of impatient husbands ignored police barricades and rushed to greet their wives and children.

The *Queen Mary* had a rigid schedule to maintain and thus stayed in Halifax only long enough to top off her fuel and fresh water tanks. She put to sea once again just after noon on May 9th and, after a brief stop in New York to embark passengers bound for Britain, set a course for Southampton. The *Queen* kept up her grueling UK-Halifax-New York-UK shuttle for the next four months, ferrying an average of 2,200 war brides and children to Canada on each west-bound crossing and returning to the United Kingdom with some 2,000 passengers on the east-bound leg of the journey. By the time the liner's Canadian "bride and baby" service ended in mid-September she had transported over 18,900 dependents, carried more than 10,100 paying passengers to Britain, and steamed an additional 50,600 miles in the process.

His Majesty's Government saw no need to retain the *Queen Mary* in military service once she had completed her dependent duties, and the Ministry of War Transport therefore informed Cunard White Star that the liner would be officially demobilized upon her September 27th return to Southampton from Halifax. The shipping line's Directors were relieved to hear this news, for they realized all too well that their firm's post-war economic survival depended almost entirely on the *Queen's* rapid reconversion and return to civilian service. The French and American national lines were already threatening Cunard's traditional predominance on the lucrative North Atlantic passenger routes and the *Queen Elizabeth,* demobilized the preceding March and nearing the end of her own reconversion, would not be able to singlehandedly prevent the British line's demise. Only the speedy inauguration of the long-anticipated two ship Atlantic shuttle could save Cunard, and the sooner the *Queen Mary* joined her younger sister on such service, the better.

The *Queen Mary's* final military voyage began in Halifax on September 24th when, just after noon, a flotilla of tugboats eased the huge vessel away from her pier and into the harbor's main channel. Captain Gordon Illingsworth ordered SLOW AHEAD rung up on the ship's engine order telegraphs, and the Cunarder moved majestically toward the open sea as thousands of watching Canadians cheered. The *Queen* returned the salute with a series of almost deafening siren blasts, then began to pick up speed as she passed the breakwater. Once clear of the harbor Captain Illingsworth ordered all engines FULL AHEAD and set a direct course for Southampton. The liner, carrying only her 993 man crew, fairly lept ahead as though she realized the significance of this final military voyage. After nearly six and a half years of faithful and constant service to King and Country, six and a half years of danger, privation and hardship, the *Queen* and the men who sailed her were finally homeward bound.

English war brides get their first look at the Statue of Liberty from the deck of the Queen Mary, *March 1946.*
The Wrather Corporation

Britons returning to Southampton aboard the Queens *received a warm welcome as well.*
Public Archives of Canada (#PA 113769)

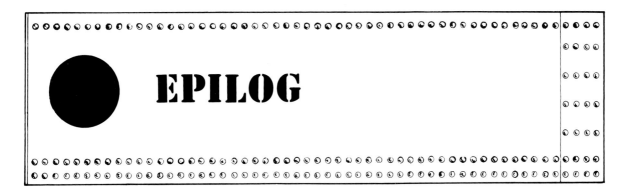

EPILOG

The *Queen Mary's* demobilization at Southampton on September 27, 1946 marked the end of a military career that had lasted nearly 79 months. And what a career it had been! While on His Majesty's Service the Cunarder and her crew had travelled over 600,000 miles, transported almost 800,000 human beings and played a major role in virtually every Allied campaign of the Second World War. In the course of her duties the *Queen* had become the first ship in history to carry 10,000 people at one time, the first ship in history to transport an entire American military division on one crossing, and the *only* ship in history ever to embark more than 16,500 persons on a single voyage. Though hunted by the combined forces of Germany, Italy and Japan the liner was never attacked, never fired her guns in anger and, most importantly, never lost a single passenger to enemy action.

And now, with her military service at an end, the *Queen Mary* was finally free to return to the North Atlantic as a ship of peace. But six and a half years of hard and constant use had wreaked havoc on the once immaculate liner and, like the *Queen Elizabeth* before her, she would require a complete renovation prior to resuming regular service. This refurbishment began in Southampton within ten days of the *Mary's* demobilization, and for the next ten months some 4,000 workers labored night and day to erase the scars left on the Cunarder by her wartime experiences. The liner's public rooms and passenger cabins were completely reconditioned, her decks and railing were resurfaced, and her rust-streaked coat of camouflage gray was replaced by Cunard's familiar red, white and black livery. During a three-week stay in the huge King George V graving dock the *Queen* finally received a proper stem to replace the temporary one installed in Boston following the *Curacao* tragedy, while at the same time her hull was scraped and her powerful but long overworked engines underwent their first comprehensive overhaul since 1939. By the time the *Queen Mary* emerged from her refit in July, 1947, she had been thoroughly refurbished inside and out, and could once again rightfully claim the title of "Stateliest Ship Afloat."

The Cunard Queens inaugurated their long-awaited Southampton-New York shuttle service in the summer of 1947, and for the next twenty years they remained the undisputed monarchs of the North Atlantic passenger trade. Their speed, elegance and luxury made them the standard by which all other express liners had to be measured and, despite the appearance of newer and larger competitors, the *Queen Mary* and *Queen Elizabeth* seemed destined for long and profitable careers. But technological progress, like time, marches inexorably onward, and by the mid-1960s the increasing popularity of international air travel had sounded the death knell for the great trans-Atlantic steamships. One after another the world's merchant fleets, faced by rising costs and plummeting revenues, dropped out of the maritime passenger trade and retired their liners. Cunard was certainly not immune to this sad trend, and by 1966 was losing some $2 million a year on the Queens. In 1967, confronted by the spectre of financial ruin, the Company reluctantly put both its superships up for sale.

For several months it seemed as though the *Queen Mary* and *Queen Elizabeth* were destined to end their lives as just so much scrap metal. They were far too large to be of any practical value in the booming cruise ship trade, and the only other alternative appeared to be the breaker's yard. But, fortunately, both liners were eventually purchased by organizations dedicated to saving them from the cutter's torch. The *Elizabeth*, bought by a group of Hong Kong businessmen, was to become a sea-going university,* while the *Mary* was obtained by the city of Long Beach, California, for use as a floating hotel and entertainment complex.

The story of the *Queen Mary's* career as a southern California landmark is a fascinating tale in itself, and has been well told elsewhere. Suffice it to say that the liner has hosted some 12 million visitors since her 1971 debut in Long Beach, and shows every sign of remaining a popular attraction for many years to come. It is indeed a fitting retirement for the ship that in peacetime became famous as the Queen of the North Atlantic, and in time of war became legendary as the Gray Ghost.

The Queen Elizabeth's *luck unfortunately did not last. The liner, renamed S.S. Seawise University by her new owners, was destroyed by fire in 1972 while undergoing conversion in Hong Kong.*

The end of a distinguished military career: His Majesty's Transport Queen Mary *returns to Southampton at the end of her final military voyage, September 27, 1946. The already civilianized* Queen Elizabeth *is visible at center left.*

"Stateliest Ship Afloat" once again. The RMS Queen Mary *in her postwar livery.*   The Cunard Line

The Queen Mary *in graceful and well-deserved retirement, Long Beach, California.*   The Wrather Corporation

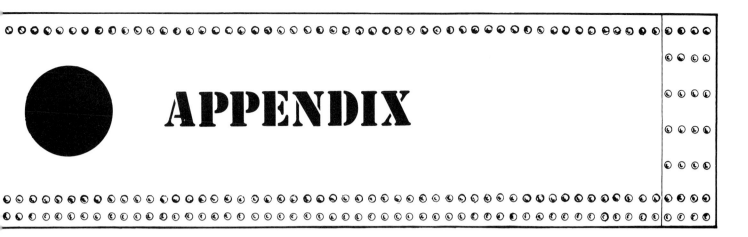

APPENDIX

I. **Wartime Specifications, HMT** *Queen Mary:*

DATES OF MILITARY SERVICE: *March 1940 to September 1946*
OVERALL LENGTH: *1019.5 feet*
MOULDED BREADTH: *118 feet*
HEIGHT (KEEL TO TOP OF FORWARD FUNNEL): *181 feet*
GROSS TONNAGE: *81,237. (This is the commonly quoted figure, though it should be taken as approximate.)*
POWERPLANTS: *24 oil-fired watertube boilers in four boiler rooms provided steam to four sets of single-reduction geared turbines. These turbines developed a total of 160,000 shaft horsepower, and drove four 35 ton screws. A fifth boiler of the smaller "Scotch" type was housed in a smaller fifth boiler room, and was used to supply auxiliary power for lighting, refrigeration, etc.*

FUEL CONSUMPTION: *Approximately 1000 tons of fuel oil every 24 hours, depending on ship's speed, weather conditions, etc.*
MAXIMUM SERVICE SPEED: *Approximately 29 knots, again depending on sea state, course, and so on.*
AVERAGE WARTIME CREW:
  Ship's Company: 850–910 officers and men.
  Permanent Military Staff: 120–140 officers and men.
TROOP/PASSENGER CAPACITY:
  As originally designed: 2030
  Maximum wartime capacity: 15,740
CARGO CAPACITY: *Approximately 45,000 cubic feet in normal holds, plus whatever could be carried on deck.*
  be carried on deck.
FRESH WATER CAPACITY:
  As originally designed: 468 tons
  Maximum wartime capacity: 6500 tons
ARMAMENT:
  1940–1942: 1 four-inch gun, plus several WW I vintage Lewis and Vickers machineguns.
  1942–1945: 1 six-inch gun
       5 three-inch high/low angle guns
       10 40mm cannon in five double mounts
       24 20mm cannon in single mounts
       4 .50 caliber Browning heavy machineguns
       4 two-inch anti-aircraft rocket launchers
       plus: assorted rifles, pistols, flareguns, etc.
RADAR: *The Queen Mary was equipped with a medium range surface-search RADAR unit during her 1942 refit in Boston.*
SONAR: *The early ASDIC-type underwater sound detection unit installed on the ship in New York in 1940 proved impractical due to the great amount of noise generated by the liner's movement through the water, and was thus rarely used.*

II. Military Voyages of HMT *Queen Mary*

This chart was compiled from information contained in the Queen Mary's *Wartime Passages Book, Sir James Bisset's book "Commodore: War, Peace and Big Ships," and from a log kept during the war by Colonel Dallas D. Dennis of the New York Port of Embarkation. The author wishes to extend sincere thanks to the staff of the Queen Mary Tour in Long Beach, California, for their assistance in obtaining this information.*

VOYAGE	ROUTE	DATES	CAPTAIN	TROOPS(T) PASSENGERS(P) CREW(C)	MILEAGE	PASSAGE TIME	AVERAGE SPEED
WW#1	New York-Trinidad	3/21/40-3/24/40	Irving		1,962	3-00-45	26.97k
	Trinidad-Cape Town	3/25/40-4/3/40	Irving		5,332	8-19-42	25.19k
	Cape Town-Freemantle	4/4/40-4/11/40	Irving		4,808	7-12-53	28.13k
	Freemantle-Sydney	4/13/40-4/17/40	Irving		2,252	3-06-42	28.61k
WW#2	Sydney-Freemantle	5/4/40-5/10/40	Irving		2,383	5-05-11	19.06k
	Freemantle-Cape Town	5/12/40-5/26/40	Irving		6,158	14-00-51	18.28k
	Capetown-Simonstown	5/28/40-5/28/40	Irving		83	0-05-45	14.43k
	Simonstown-Freetown	5/31/40-6/7-40	Irving		3,267	7-03-47	19.04k
	Freetown-Clyde	6/8/40-6/16/40	Irving		3,443	7-17-20	18.57k
WW#3	Clyde-Freetown	6/29/40-7/8/40	Irving		4,233	9-00-42	19.60k
	Freetown-Cape Town	7/9/40-7/16/40	Irving		3,507	6-19-36	21.43k
	Cape Town-Simonstown	7/17/40-7/17/40	Irving		85	0-04-13	20.19k
	S'town-Trincomalee	7/19/40-7/29/40	Irving		4,744	9-11-50	20.82k
	T'mali-Singapore	8/1/40-8/4/40	Irving		1,582	2-14-41	25.23k
	DRYDOCK: Singapore, 8/5/40-9/16/40						
	Signapore-Sydney	9/18/40-9/25/40	Irving		4,597	6-21-40	27.74k
WW#4	Sydney-Freemantle	10/20/40-10/24/40	Irving		2,296	4-22-12	19.45k
	Freemantle-Bombay	10/26/40-11/4/40	Irving		4,054	8-03-32	20.84k
	Bombay-Freemantle	11/9/40-11/15/40	Irving		4,122	6-00-12	28.58k
	Freemantle-Sydney	11/16/40-11/21/40	Irving		2,550	4-02-16	25.95k
WW#5	Sydney-Freemantle	12/28/40-1/3/41	Irving		2,697	6-02-25	18.42k
	Freemantle-T'mali	1/4/41-1/12/41	Irving		3,191	7-01-07	18.87k
	T'mali-Freemantle	1/14/41-1/19/41	Irving		3,169	5-00-16	26.35k
	Freemantle-Sydney	1/20/41-1/24/41	Irving		2,557	3-22-35	27.04k
WW#6	Sydney-Freemantle	2/4/41-2/9/41	Irving		2,740	5-18-48	19.74k
	F'mantle-Signapore	2/12/41-2/18/41	Irving		2,495	5-18-54	17.96k
	DRYDOCK: Signapore, 2/21/41-3/1/41						
	S'pore-Freemantle	3/22/41-3/26/41	Irving		2,494	4-00-08	25.94k
	Freemantle-Sydney	3/28/41-4/1/41	Irving		2,371	3-20-08	25.74k
WW#7	Sydney-Jervis Bay	4/9/41-4/9/41	Fall		119	0-05-08	23.18k
	J. Bay-Freemantle	4/11/41-4/16/41	Fall		2,256	4-23-46	18.84k
	F'mantle-T'mali	4/19/41-4/26/41	Fall		3,456	6-23-48	20.59k
	Trincomalee-Suez	4/27/41-5/3/41	Fall		3,752	5-23-55	26.09k
	Suez-Trincomalee	5/7/41-5/14/41	Fall		3,772	6-08-51	24.67k
	T'mali-Freemantle	5/25/41-5/21/41	Fall		3,158	5-14-15	23.50k
	Freemantle-Sydney	5/21/41-5/25/41	Fall		2,328	3-23-00	24.50k
WW#8	Sydney-Hobart	6/13/41-6/14/41	Irving		678	1-03-12	24.93k
	Hobart-Sydney	6/27/41-6/28/41	Irving		664	1-02-28	25.25k
	Sydney-Freemantle	6/29/41-7/4/41	Irving		2,567	5-13-43	19.20k
	F'mantle-T'mali	7/9/41-7/16/41	Irving		3,162	6-16-52	19.64k
	Trincomalee-Suez	7/17/41-7/25/41	Irving		3,795	7-13-27	20.91k
	Suez-Trincomalee	7/26/41-8/2/41	Irving		3,791	6-08-29	24.84k
	T'mali-Freemantle	8/4/41-8/9/41	Irving		3,176	5-12-54	23.90k
	Freemantle-Sydney	8/10/41-8/15/41	Irving		2,329	4-04-12	23.24k

VOYAGE	ROUTE	DATES	CAPTAIN	TROOPS(T) PASSENGERS(P) CREW(C)	MILEAGE	PASSAGE TIME	AVERAGE SPEED
WW#9	Sydney-Hobart	8/21/41-8/23/41	Irving		677	1-03-15	24.84k
	Hobart-Sydney	9/1/41-9/2/41	Irving		675	1-04-18	23.85k
	Sydney-Freemantle	9/3/41-9/7/41	Irving		2,315	4-16-16	20.62k
	F'mantle-T'mali	9/9/41-9/15/41	Irving		3,162	5-10-00	24.32k
	Trincomalee-Suez	9/16/41-9/23/41	Irving		3,786	6-19-58	23.09k
	Suez-Trincomalee	9/24/41-10/1/41	Irving		3,795	6-09-12	24.77k
	T'mali-Freemantle	10/1/41-10/7/41	Irving		3,200	5-13-45	23.93k
	Freemantle-Sydney	10/8/41-10/13/41	Irving		2,587	4-18-48	22.53k
WW#10	Sydney-Hobart	10/15/41-10/16/41	Irving		699	1-03-45	24.24k
	Hobart-Sydney	10/22/41-10/23/41	Irving		685	1-03-51	24.68k
	Sydney-Jervis Bay	11/1/41-11/2/41	Townley		108	0-05-30	19.64k
	J. Bay-Freemantle	11/2/41-11/6/41	Townley		2,352	4-00-56	24.45k
	F'mantle-T'mali	11/8/41-11/14/41	Townley		3,179	5-15-48	23.64k
	Trincomalee-Suez	11/15/41-11/22/41	Townley		3,835	6-20-45	23.86k
	Suez-Trincomalee	11/23/41-11/30/41	Townley		3,783	6-12-15	24.22k
	T'mali-Cape Town	12/19/41-12/28/41	Townley		5,100	8-16-18	24.48k
WW#11	Cape Town-Trinidad	12/29/41-1/8/42	Townley		5,368	10-00-18	22.34k
	Trinidad-New York	1/8/42-1/12/42	Townley		1,959	3-11-30	23.66k
	New York-Boston	1/26/42-1/27/42	Townley		385	0-16-34	23.22k
	DRYDOCK: Boston Naval Shipyard, 1/27/42-2/8/42						
WW#12	Boston-Key West	2/18/42-2/22/42	Townley		2,369	3-21-27	25.35k
	Key West-Rio	2/24/42-3/6/42	Bisset	8398(T),905(C) (To Sydney)	5,589	9-14-57	24.20k
	Rio-Cape Town	3/8/42-3/14/42	Bisset		3,383	5-07-39	26.50k
	C'town-Freemantle	3/15/42-3/23/42	Bisset		4,801	7-15-08	26.22k
	Freemantle-Sydney	3/24/42-3/28/42	Bisset		2,356	3-21-02	25.61k
WW#13	Sydney-Freemantle	4/6/42-4/11/42	Bisset	58(P),832(C)	2,800	5-03-20	22.70k
	F'mantle-Cape Town	4/12/42-4/21/42	Bisset		5,142	8-20-39	24.18k
	Cape Town-Rio	4/22/42-4/27/42	Bisset		3,311	5-04-32	26.51k
	Rio-New York	4/28/42-5/7/42	Bisset		5,283	8-16-03	25.39k
WW#14	New York-Clyde	5/11/42-5/16/42	Bisset	9880(T),875(C)	3,166	5-03-45	25.58k
	(Note: This marked the first time in history that 10,000 persons had voyaged in one ship.)						
WW#15	Clyde-Freetown	5/22/42-5/30/42	Bisset	9537(T)(To Suez) 872(C)	4,137	7-10-52	23.13k
	F'town-Cape Town	5/31/42-6/6/42	Bisset		3,423	5-14-06	25.52k
	C'town-Simonstown	6/8/42-6/8/42	Bisset		84	0-03-09	26.66k
	Simonstown-Suez	6/10/42-6/22/42	Bisset		5,998	11-10-11	21.88k
	Suez-Simonstown	6/23/42-7/5/42	Bisset	2565(P),871(C)	5,930	11-19-38	20.92k
	Simonstown-Rio	7/7/42-7/12/42	Bisset		3,290	5-01-48	27.01k
	Rio-New York	7/13/42-7/21/42	Bisset		4,980	7-17-15	26.88k
WW#16	New York-Gourock	8/2/42-8/7/42	Bisset	15,125(T),863(C)	3,266	5-02-00	26.77k
	(Note: This marked the first time in history an entire U.S. division voyaged in one ship.)						
WW#17W	Gourock-New York	8/11/42-8/16/42	Illingsworth		3,554	5-08-29	27.66k
WW#17E	New York-Gourock	9/5/42-9/11/42	Illingsworth		3,631	5-09-39	28.01k
WW#18W	Gourock-New York	9/14/42-9/19/42	Illingsworth		3,581	5-15-11	26.49k
WW#18E	New York-Gourock	9/27/42-10/3/42	Illingsworth		3,294	5-10-46	25.19k
WW#19W	Gourock-Boston	10/8/42-10/14/42	Illingsworth		3,387	6-13-43	21.47k
	DRYDOCK: Boston Naval Shipyard, 10/14/42-11/2/42						
	Boston-New York	11/4/42-11/5/42	Illingsworth		490	0-21-02	23.30k
WW#19E	New York-Gourock	12/8/42-12/14/42	Bisset	10,389(T),950(C)	3,677	6-00-37	25.42k

VOYAGE	ROUTE	DATES	CAPTAIN	TROOPS(T) PASSENGERS(P) CREW(C)	MILEAGE	PASSAGE TIME	AVERAGE SPEED
WW#20	Gourock-Freetown	12/23/42-12/29/42	Bisset	10,669(T) (To Massawa),800(C)	3,897	6-09-37	25.37k
	F'town-Cape Town	12/30/42-1/5/43	Bisset		3,441	5-18-00	24.93k
	Cape Town-Aden	1/7/43-1/15/43	Bisset		4,981	8-04-45	25.31k
	Aden-Suez	1/15/43-1/18/43	Bisset		1,332	2-10-00	22.96k
	Suez-Massawa	1/25/43-1/28/43	Bisset	9,995(T) (To Sydney),877(C)	1,050	2-18-42	15.74k
	Massawa-Maldive Is.	2/3/43-2/9/43	Bisset		2,556	6-06-00	17.04k
	Maldive Is-F'mantle	2/10/43-2/18/43	Bisset		3,149	7-20-30	16.71k
	Freemantle-Sydney	2/20/43-2/27/43	Bisset		2,881	6-15-54	18.02k
	Sydney-Freemantle	3/22/43-3/26/43	Bisset	8,326(T) (To Gourock),874(C)	2,681	4-08-42	28.60k
	F'mantle-Cape Town	3/28/43-4/6/43	Bisset		4,903	9-01-21	22.55k
	C'town-Freetown	4/9/43-4/15/43	Bisset		3,446	5-18-00	24.97k
	Freetown-Gourock	4/16/43-4/22/43	Bisset		3,626	6-02-03	24.83k
WW#21W	Gourock-New York	5/5/43-5/11/43	Irving		3,489	5-20-50	24.78k
	DRYDOCK: Bayonne, N.J., 5/13/43-5/19/43						
WW#21E	New York-Gourock	6/1/43-6/6/43	Irving		3,469	5-07-33	27.19k
WW#22W	Gourock-New York	6/10/43-6/16/43	Bisset	6,235(P),922(C)	3,358	5-13-24	25.13k
WW#22E	New York-Gourock	6/24/43-6/29/43	Bisset	15,281(T),927(C)	3,327	4-23-18	27.88k
WW#23W	Gourock-New York	7/4/43-7/9/43	Bisset	4,427(P),908(C)	3,203	5-01-24	26.39k
WW#23E	New York-Gourock	7/23/43-7/30/43	Bisset	15,740(T),943(C)	3,231	4-20-42	27.69k
	(Note: This marks the greatest number of human beings ever embarked on a single ocean crossing.)						
WW#24W	Gourock-New York	8/5/43-8/9/43	Bisset	2,305(P), 1,036(C)	2,563	4-03-42	25.71k
WW#24E	New York-Gourock	8/27/43-8/31/43	Bisset	15,116(T),937(C)	2,607	3-23-18	27.36k
WW#25W	Gourock-New York	9/5/43-9/10/43	Illingsworth		3,187	5-08-48	24.74k
	DRYDOCK: Bayonne, N.J., 9/11/43-9/16/43						
WW#25E	New York-Gourock	9/20/43-9/25/43	Illingsworth		3,105	4-18-42	27.07k
WW#26W	Gourock-New York	9/29/43-10/5/43	Illingsworth		3,434	5-13-18	25.76k
WW#26E	New York-Gourock	10/9/43-10/15/43	Illingsworth		3,631	5-15-33	26.79k
WW#27W	Gourock-New York	10/18/43-10/24/43	Illingsworth		3,466	5-10-07	26.64k
WW#27E	New York-Gourock	10/24/43-11/2/43	Illingsworth		3,408	5-07-36	26.71k
WW#28W	Gourock-New York	11/5/43-11/11/43	Bisset	1,475(P),903(C)	3,683	5-17-54	26.71k
WW#28E	New York-Gourock	11/15/43-11/20/43	Bisset	12,146(T),904(C)	3,120	4-18-00	27.37k
WW#29W	Gourock-New York	11/24/43-11/30/43	Bisset	1,203(P),910(C)	3,222	5-01-30	26.52k
WW#29E	New York-Gourock	12/3/43-12/9/43	Bisset	11,907(T), 1,080(C)	3,540	5-11-12	26.98k
WW#30W	Gourock-New York	12/4/43-12/20/43	Bisset	2,847(P), 1,087(C)	3,635	5-15-36	26.81k
WW#30E	New York-Gourock	12/23/43-12/29/43	Bisset	11,990(T) 1,087(C)	3,662	5-10-30	28.06k
WW#31W	Gourock-New York	1/3/44-1/9/44	Illingsworth		3,735	6-02-04	25.57k
WW#31E	New York-Guorock	1/22/44-1/28/44	Illingsworth		3,714	5-20-28	26.44k
WW#32W	Gourock-New York	1/31/44-2/6/44	Illingsworth		3,502	5-17-18	25.51k
WW#32E	New York-Gourock	2/12/44-2/18/44	Illingsworth		3,767	5-22-06	26.51k
WW#33W	Gourock-New York	2/21/44-2/27/44	Bisset	1,332(P), 940(C)	3,340	5-11-54	25.32k
WW#33E	New York-Gourock	3/1/44-3/7/44	Bisset	11,950(T), 1,190(C)	3,504	5-12-12	26.51k

VOYAGE	ROUTE	DATES	CAPTAIN	TROOPS(T) PASSENGERS(P) CREW(C)	MILEAGE	PASSAGE TIME	AVERAGE SPEED
WW#34W	Gourock-New York	3/11/44-3/17/44	Bisset	2,042(P), 1,123(C)	3.456	5-13-06	25.97k
WW#34E	New York-Gourock	3/21/44-3/27/44	Bisset	12,072(T), 1,099(C)	3,603	5-15-36	26.57k
WW#35W	Gourock-New York	3/31/44-4/6/44	Bisset	1,246(P), 1,091(C)	3,607	5-17-30	26.33k
WW#35E	New York-Gourock	4/10/44-4/16/44	Bisset	11,979(T), 1,086(C)	3,909	6-03-12	26.57k
WW#36W	Gourock-New York	5/7/44-5/13/44	Bisset	968(P), 935(C)	3,668	5-19-24	26.31k
WW#36E	New York-Gourock	6/7/44-6/13/44	Bisset	11,993(T), 1,112(C)	3,561	5-12-18	26.92k
WW#37W	Gourock-New York	6/17/44-6/23/44	Bisset	4,898(P), 1,103(C)	3,470	5-09-42	26.75k
WW#37E	New York-Gourock	7/1/44-7/7/44	Bisset	14,533(T), 1,105(C)	3,434	5-07-54	26.85k
WW#38W	Gourock-New York	7/11/44-7/17/44	Bisset	5,060(P), 1,102(C)	3,447	5-14-12	25.69k
WW#38E	New York-Gourock	7/23/44-7/28/44	Bisset	12,009(T), 1,130(C)	3,315	4-22-18	28.02k
WW#39W	Gourock-New York	8/6/44-8/12/44	Spencer		3,260	5-05-21	26.01k
WW#39E	New York-Gourock	8/20/44-8/26/44	Spencer		3,615	5-16-06	26.56k
WW#40W	Gourock-Halifax	9/5/44-9/10/44	Bisset	3,594(P), 1,107(C)	3,100	4-19-12	26.91k
	Halifax-New York	9/10/44-9/11/44	Bisset		650	0-23-18	27.90k
WW#40E	New York-Gourock	9/20/44-9/25/44	Bisset	9,084(T), 1,110(C)	3,412	5-00-00	28.43k
WW#41W	Gourock-New York	10/2/44-10/8/44	Bisset	5,047(P), 1,086(C)	3,597	5-11-30	27.35k
WW#41E	New York-Gourock	10/12/44-10/18/44	Bisset	11,891(T), 1,061(C)	3,499	5-08-54	27.15k
WW#42W	Gourock-New York	10/22/44-10/28/44	Bisset	3,016(P), 1,059(C)	3,679	5-16-12	27.01k
WW#42E	New York-Gourock	11/3/44-11/9/44	Bisset	11,968(T), 1,065(C)	3,558	5-10-12	27.33k
WW#43W	Gourock-New York	11/13/44-11/19/44	Bisset	2,477(P), 1,076(C)	3,485	5-20-24	24.82k
	DRYDOCK: Bayonne, N.J., 11/20/44-12/7/44						
WW#43E	New York-Gourock	12/10/44-12/16/44	Bisset	11,996(T), 1,084(C)	3,595	5-10-18	27.59k
WW#44W	Gourock-New York	12/21/44-12/27/44	Illingsworth		3,508	5-11-20	26.71k
WW#44E	New York-Gourock	1/1/45-1/7/45	Illingsworth		3,641	5-16-44	26.63k
WW#45W	Gourock-New York	1/13/45-1/19/45	Irving		3,487	5-13-20	26.15k
WW#45E	New York-Gourock	1/24/45-1/30/45	Irving		3,645	5-15-30	26.90k
WW#46W	Gourock-New York	2/5/45-2/11/45	Bisset	3,293(P), 1,140(C)	3,387	5-22-24	23.79k
WW#46E	New York-Gourock	2/19/45-2/24/45	Bisset	11,226(T), 1,382(C)	3,463	5-01-54	28.41k
WW#47W	Gourock-New York	3/5/45-3/11/45	Bisset	4,111(P), 1,366(C)	3,630	5-14-36	26.97k
WW#47E	New York-Gourock	3/18/45-3/23/45	Bisset	10,905(T), 1,385(C)	3,426	5-02-30	27.96k

VOYAGE	ROUTE	DATES	CAPTAIN	TROOPS(T) PASSENGERS(P) CREW(C)	MILEAGE	PASSAGE TIME	AVERAGE SPEED
WW#48W	Gourock-New York	3/29/45-4/4/45	Bisset	3,895(P), 1,387(C)	3,750	5-20-18	26.73k
	DRYDOCK: Bayonne, N.J., 4/18/45-4/19/45						
WW#48E	New York-Gourock	6/5/45-6/10/45	Bisset	1,207(P), 1,026(C)	3,264	4-17-00	28.88k
WW#49W	Gourock-New York	6/15/45-6/20/45	Bisset	14,777(T), 893(C)	3,202	4-21-48	27.18k
WW#49E	New York-Gourock	6/26/45-7/1/45	Bisset	1,040(P), 903(C)	3,205	4-19-18	27.80k
WW#50W	Gourock-New York	7/6/45-7/11/45	Irving	8,551(T), 12(P)	3,291	4-21-38	27.98k
WW#50E	New York-Gourock	7/17/45-7/22/45	Irving	567(T)	3,202	4-13-48	29.20k
WW#51W	Gourock-New York	7/28/45-8/2/45	Illingsworth	14,790(T), 68(P)	3,136	4-14-08	28.49k
WW#51E	New York-Southampton	8/6/45-8/11/45	Illingsworth	643(T), 68(P)	3,250	4-22-00	27.55k
WW#52W	Southampton-New York	8/17/45-8/21/45	Illingsworth	14,776(T), 58(P)	3,157	4-15-24	28.34k
WW#52E	New York-Southampton	8/26/45-8/31/45	Illingsworth	11(T), 93(P)	3,175	4-22-59	26.69k
WW#53W	Southampton-New York	9/5/45-9/10/45	Fall	14,803(T), 88(P)	3,137	4-19-40	27.12k
WW#53E	New York-Southampton	9/13/45-9/18/45	Fall	54(T), 31(P)	3,172	5-00-54	26.24k
WW#54W	Southampton-New York	9/23/45-9/28/45	Fall	14,938(T), 161(P), 834(C)	3,131	4-20-40	26.84k
WW#54E	New York-Southampton	10/1/45-10/7/45	Fall	11(T), 29(P)	3,167	5-11-42	24.05k
WW#55W	Southampton-New York	10/11/45-10/16/45	Fall	11,383(T), 202(P), 836(C)	3,134	4-22-54	26.36k
WW#55E	New York-Southampton	10/20/45-10/25/45	Fall		3,173	5-10-09	24.38k
WW#56W	Southampton-New York	11/4/45-11/9/45	Fall	11,483(T), 48(P), 837(C)	3,116	4-16-22	27.73k
WW#56E	New York-Southampton	11/13/45-11/18/45	Fall	4,540(P), 836(C)	3,159	4-12-55	29.01k
WW#57W	Southampton-New York	11/22/45-11/27/45	Fall	11,683(T), 843(C)	3,136	4-22-18	26.51k
WW#57E	New York-Southampton	11/30/45-12/6/45	Fall	1,200(P), 843(C)	3,163	5-09-48	24.37k
WW#58W	Southampton-New York	12/09/45-12/14/45	Fall	11,588(T), 846(C)	3,134	4-22-41	26.41k
WW#58E	New York-Southampton	12/18/45-12/23/45	Fall	1,201(P), 842(C)	3,167	4-22-30	26.73k
WW#59W	Southampton-New York	12/29/45-1/3/46	Illingsworth	11,346(T), 846(C)	3,136	5-01-34	25.80k
WW#59E	New York-Southampton	1/6/46-1/11/46	Illingsworth	1,078(P), 845(C)	3,174	4-23-27	26.57k
	DRYDOCK: Southampton, 1/14/46-1/30/46						
WW#60W	Southampton-New York	2/5/46-2/10/46	Illingsworth	2,509(P), 943(C)	3,137	5-23-12	21.91k
WW#60E	New York-Southampton	2/17/46-2/21/46	Illingsworth	1,793(P), 944(C)	3,174	4-21-30	27.01k
WW#61W	Southampton-New York	2/25/46-3/1/46	Illingsworth	2,489(P), 935(C)	3,137	4-23-39	26.23k
WW#61E	New York-Southampton	3/5/46-3/9/46	Illingsworth		3,174	4-17-57	27.85k
WW#62W	Southampton-New York	3/13/46-3/18/46	Ford		3,135	4-21-57	26.70k
WW#62E	New York-Southampton	3/21/46-3/26/46	Ford		3,171	4-23-10	26.63k
WW#63W	Southampton-New York	3/31/46-4/4/46	Ford		3,212	5-01-20	26.48k
WW#63E	New York-Southampton	4/8/46-4/12/46	Ford	1,328(P), 936(C)	3,242	4-19-09	28.15k
WW#64W	Southampton-New York	4/17/46-4/21/46	Ford	2,509(P), 943(C)	3,202	4-21-00	27.37k
WW#64E	New York-Southampton	4/25/46-4/30/46	Ford	1,582(P), 941(C)	3,277	4-22-34	27.63k

VOYAGE	ROUTE	DATES	CAPTAIN	TROOPS(T) PASSENGERS(P) CREW(C)	MILEAGE	PASSAGE TIME	AVERAGE SPEED
WW#65W	Southampton-Halifax	5/5/46-5/8/46	Ford	2,495(P), 957(C)	2,735	4-02-00	27.91k
	Halifax-New York	5/9/46-5/10/46	Ford		577	1-00-22	23.68k
WW#65E	New York-Southampton	5/14/46-5/19/46	Ford	1,617(P), 979(C)	3,242	4-21-34	27.58k
WW#66W	Southampton-Halifax	5/24/46-5/27/46	Illingsworth	2,488(P), 977(C)	2,710	4-00-23	28.12k
	Halifax-New York	5/29/46-5/29/46	Illingsworth		572	0-21-30	26.60k
WW#66E	New York-Southampton	6/2/46-6/6/46	Illingsworth	1,330(P), 977(C)	3,225	4-18-50	28.09k
WW#67W	Southampton-Halifax	6/11/46-6/15/46	Illingsworth	2,482(P), 990(C)	2,739	4-01-57	27.96k
	Halifax-New York	6/16/46-6/17/46	Illingsworth		572	0-22-30	25.42k
WW#67E	New York-Southampton	6/21/46-6/26/46	Illingsworth	1,323(P), 987(C)	3,236	4-23-35	27.06k
WW#68W	Southampton-Halifax	7/1/46-7/4/46	Illingsworth	2,543(P), 993(C)	2,728	4-01-23	28.01k
	Halifax-New York	7/5/46-7/6/46	Illingsworth		572	0-22-55	24.95k
WW#68E	New York-Southampton	7/10/46-7/14/46	Illingsworth	1,217(P), 1,006(C)	3,226	4-18-06	28.27k
WW#69W	Southampton-Halifax	7/20/46-7/23/46	Illingsworth		2,716	4-01-43	27.79k
	Halifax-New York	7/24/46-7/25/46	Illingsworth		572	0-21-31	26.58k
WW#69E	New York-Southampton	7/29/46-8/2/46	Illingsworth		3,162	4-17-46	27.79k
WW#70W	Southampton-Halifax	8/8/46-8/11/46	Ford	2,428(P), 994(C)	2,659	3-23-19	27.89k
	Halifax-New York	8/13/46-8/13/46	Ford		572	0-21-40	26.40k
WW#70E	New York-Southampton	8/17/46-8/21/46	Ford	1,419(P), 1,018(C)	3,164	4-19-00	27.51k
WW#71W	Southampton-Halifax	8/28/46-8/31/46	Illingsworth	2,370(P), 995(C)	2,657	4-06-30	25.92k
	Halifax-New York	9/2/46-9/3/46	Illingsworth		572	1-00-16	23.57k
WW#71E	New York-Southampton	9/6/46-9/10/46	Illingsworth	1,455(P), 972(C)	3,160	4-17-05	27.94k
WW#72W	Southampton-Halifax	9/15/46-9/18/46	Illingsworth	2,077(P), 993(C)	2,561	4-00-55	26.42k
WW#72E	Halifax-Southampton	9/24/46-9/27/46	Illingsworth	993(C)	2,531	3-15-48	28.83k

Note: The *Queen Mary* was demobilized at Southampton on 27 September 1946.

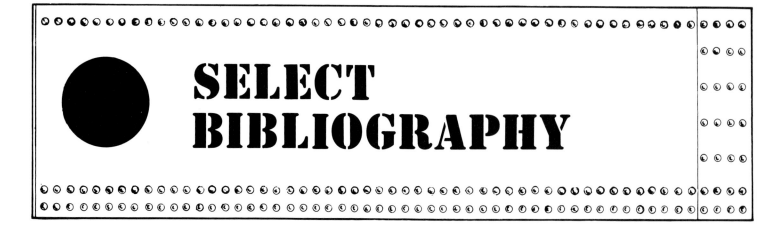

SELECT BIBLIOGRAPHY

Behrens, C.B.A. *Merchant Shipping and the Demands of War.* In the series *History of the Second World: United Kingdom Civil Series.* London: Her Majesty's Stationery Office, 1978.

Bisset, Sir James. *Commodore; War, Peace and Big Ships.* London: Angus Robertson, LTD, 1961.

Brinnin, John Malcolm. *The Sway of the Grand Salon.* New York: Delacorte Press, 1971.

Bykofsky, Joseph, and Larson, Harold. *The Transportation Corps: Operations Overseas.* In the series *United States Army in World War II.* Washington, D.C.: Office of the Chief of Military History, 1957.

Charles, Roland W. *Troopships of World War II.* Washington, D.C.: Army Transportation Association, 1947.

Duncan, William J. *RMS Queen Mary: Queen of the Queens.* Anderson, S.C.: Droke House, 1969.

Grattidge, Captain Harry. *Captain of the Queens.* New York: E.P. Dutton & Co., 1956.

Ismay, General Lord. *Memoirs of General Lord Ismay.* New York: Viking Press, 1960.

Lacey, Robert. *The Queens of the North Atlantic.* London: Sidgwick & Jackson, 1978.

Maxton-Graham, John. *The Only Way to Cross.* New York: The MacMillan Company, 1972.

Mueller, Edward A. *The Stateliest Ship.* Staten Island, New York: The Steamship Historical Society, 1969.

Potter, Neil, and Frost, Jack. *The Queen Mary: Her Inception and History.* San Francisco: San Francisco Press, 1971.

_____. *The Elizabeth.* San Francisco: San Francisco Press, 1965.

ACKOWLEDGMENTS

I would like to thank the following individuals and organizations for their help in researching the military history of the *Queen Mary*. Without their valuable assistance this book would not have been possible.

In the United States:

Nick Noxon, WQED-TV, Pittsburgh, Pa.
MMCS (SS) Gary Morrison, U.S. Submarine Force Museum, Groton, Conn.
Florence Frail, Charleston, S.C.
Alice Marshall, The Cunard Line, New York, N.Y.
Jodie Davis and Dennis Mroczkowski, U.S. Army Transportation Corps Museum, Fort Eustis, Va.
SSgt John Cooley, 831st Air Division, George AFB, Calif.
JOC Bruce Blakeman, LT Mary Cullen, and David Sims, Naval Station Treasure Island, San Francisco, Calif.
The Navy and Marine Corps Museum, San Francisco, Calif.
Jeff Dixon, Australia Information Services, New York, N.Y.
Michael Curtin, The Hampton Roads Museum
Charles Haberlien, U.S. Naval Historical Center, Washington, D.C.
The Naval Education and Training Support Center, Pacific, San Diego, Calif.
The U.S. Army Military History Center, Washington, D.C.
Robert Scheina, U.S. Coast Guard Public Affairs Office, Washington, D.C.
The Prints and Photographs Divison, Library of Congress, Washington, D.C.
The Still Picture Branch, National Archives, Washington, D.C.
James Foster, The Steamship Historical Society, Baltimore, Md.
The Mariner's Museum, Newport News, Va.
The Staff, DYNAPAC Photographic, San Diego, Calif.

In the United Kingdom:

H.L. Theobald, Historical Section, The Cabinet Office, London
Michael Cook, University of Liverpool Archives
Michael Moss and Allan Macquarie, Glasgow University Archives
Allan MacKenzie, John Brown Engineering, Ltd., Clydebank
J.S. Lucas, The Imperial War Museum, London
The National Maritime Museum, Greenwich
The Naval Historical Branch, Ministry of Defence, London
The Cunard Line, Ltd., London
The Southampton City Council

In Australia:

Noel Flanagan and Michael Piggott, The Australian War Memorial, Canberra
The Australian Archives, Canberra
Shirley Humphries, The Mitchell Library, Sydney
R. Mills, The Department of Defence, Canberra

In Canada:
Joy Williams, Public Archives of Canada, Ottawa
W.A.B. Douglas, Directorate of History, National Defence Headquarters, Ottawa
Ludwig Kosche, The Canadian War Museum, Ottawa

In South Africa:
A.C. McNaught, Cape Town
Peter Humphries, Sea Point
P. Davies, Cape Town
LCDR W.M. Bisset, Office of the Chief of the South African Defence Forces, Pretoria
C.A. Kidwell, The Ship Society of South Africa, Cape Town
The Military and Maritime Museum, Castle of Good Hope, Cape Town
The South African National War Museum, Johannesburg

In West Germany:
The Bundesarchiv, Frieburg im Breisgau

In Singapore:
LTC Lee Seng Kong, Ministry of Defence, Tanglin

In Hong Kong:
A.I. Diamond and Dennis Leung, Public Records Office

In Japan:
Maritime Self Defence Force Library, Tokyo

Finally, a special thanks to Milton Schwartz and Erik Kamien of the Wrather Corporation Staff aboard the *Queen Mary*. Their unflagging support and friendship are greatly appreciated.

ABOUT THE AUTHOR

After service in the U.S. Army during the Vietnam War, Stephen Harding entered the University of California at Santa Barbara and completed both BA and MA degrees in modern military history. He is the former Director of the Navy and Marine Corps Museum in San Francisco, a former command historian in the U.S. Air Force History Program, and is currently a defense affairs journalist and author based in Washington, D.C. Mr. Harding is the author of five books on aviation, maritime and defense topics, and his articles have appeared in a range of American and European periodicals.